100 IDEAS
FOR DEVELOPING THINKING
IN THE PRIMARY SCHOOL

WEEK LOAN

CONTINUUM ONE HUNDREDS SERIES

100+ Ideas for Managing Behaviour – Johnnie Young

100+ Ideas for Teaching Creativity – Stephen Bowkett

100+ Ideas for Teaching Mathematics – Mike Ollerton

100+ Ideas for Teaching Thinking Skills – Stephen Bowkett

100+ Ideas for Teaching English – Angella Cooze

100+ Ideas for Teaching History – Julia Murphy

100 Ideas for Surviving Your First Year in Teaching – Laura-Jane Fisher

100 Ideas for Trainee Teachers – Angella Cooze

100 Ideas for Teaching Citizenship – Ian Davies

100 Ideas for Supply Teachers – Julia Murphy

100 Ideas for Teaching Science – Sharon Archer

100 Ideas for Teaching Geography – Andy Leeder

100 Ideas for Primary Supply Teachers – Michael Parry

100 Ideas for Essential Teaching Skills – Neal Watkin and Johannes Ahrenfelt

100 Ideas for Primary Assemblies – Fred Sedgwick

100 Ideas for Teaching Writing – Anthony Haynes

100 Ideas for Lesson Planning – Anthony Haynes

100 Ideas for Secondary School Assemblies – Susan Elkin

100 Ideas for Teaching Drama – Johnnie Young

100 IDEAS
FOR DEVELOPING
THINKING IN THE
PRIMARY SCHOOL

Fred Sedgwick

continuum

For Colin,
brother, friend, sparring partner
with much love and gratitude.

The unexamined life is not worth living.

The only thing we require to be good philosophers
is the faculty of wonder.

Continuum International Publishing Group

The Tower Building   80 Maiden Lane
11 York Road   Suite 704
London   New York
SE1 7NX   NY 10038

www.continuumbooks.com

British Library Cataloguing-in-Publication Data
A catalogue record for this book is available from the British
Library.

ISBN: 9780826483997 (paperback)

Designed and typeset by Ben Cracknell Studios
www.benstudios.co.uk

Printed and bound in Great Britain by MPG Books Ltd.

CONTENTS

INTRODUCTION

Jostein Gaarder's book *Sophie's World* is both a mystery novel for all ages from about eleven years upwards, and a unique introduction to philosophy. Its heroine, Sophie Amundsen, notices that, just at the point when she is beginning to become a philosopher, 'at schools . . . people were only concerned with trivialities'.

Much of the curriculum is concerned with trivia. I'm thinking of those Key Stage One topics called 'People who help us'. It doesn't get better at Key Stage Two. Much of the curriculum there is composed of important things made trivial. There are topics about Henry VIII, for example (being ditched as I write, but the point still holds), which amount to little more than copies, in paint, felt tip, line drawings, or collages, of contemporary paintings of the king and his wives. This man was a tyrant, I want to shout when I see these pictures, a murderer! Think Hitler, think Stalin. What does it matter how accurately the children can make likenesses of the king and his wives?

Children are both capable and deserving of better than that. They can think much more than we (parents, teachers and learning assistants) give them credit for. In bed at night, before they sleep, they turn big issues over in their heads. One girl in a Catholic school said to the whole class once, 'My granddad wasn't a Christian. Will he be in heaven when I go there?' (see Ideas 69–73). At school, all of them are obsessed with at least one of the great human issues, justice: 'It isn't fair,' they say.

This book is about major themes that have troubled humanity since the year dot, and it's about helping children to think purposefully, creatively and in an organized way about those major themes. 'The only thing we require to be good philosophers is the faculty of wonder.' Children have that sense. With many adults, it has become dulled. They shrug and accept, rather than think, let alone philosophize. Our job is to nurture a sense of wonder in the children. In that process, we will rediscover a sharpness in our own thinking.

A WHOLE-SCHOOL APPROACH

Everybody who has written about innovation in primary schools will say that a whole-school approach is necessary for the innovation's success. No plant will take root unless everybody is committed to watering it, feeding it, watching over it every day, and admiring it. Teaching philosophy or thinking in your classroom, and therefore treating the children as the human beings they are, already full of thoughts and ideas, will fail if, by contrast, a colleague next door is treating children as empty vessels to be filled, or clean slates to be written on. Everyone has to believe that children have that sense of wonder, and also that sense that 'the unexamined life is not worth living'.

This is a moral, as well as a curricular issue. If there isn't an agreement that children are active learners, when the children move from a teacher who is helping the children to philosophize, to a class where the 'empty vessels' teacher is teaching, they are going to be jolted, and, quite likely, intellectually and emotionally damaged. Who are they to believe? This Sir, or that Sir? That Miss, or this Miss? Both are teachers. Both have power.

Perhaps that sentence about 'the unexamined life' is better put the other way round: 'the examined life is the only one worth living.' What does it mean to examine a life? It is to question one's motives, to reflect constantly on the right road to take, and to be true to one's understanding. It is to ask, not as a rhetorical or cynical question, 'What do we mean by "peace", or "love" or "believe" or "fair" or "just"?' 'What is truth? said jesting Pilate, and would not stay for an answer.' Children want to ask the question, and wait for the answer that lurks somewhere inside themselves. 'Empty vessels' and 'clean slates' are objects, not humans, and 'to be filled' and 'to be written on' are passive, not active verbs. But thinking is active. As surely as the body does in its obvious way, the mind also moves and runs and leaps and climbs.

The curriculum is all about thinking. What can we study without it? As John Dewey famously wrote, 'Philosophy may even be defined as the general theory of education'. If we can encourage it, there is the potential for serious thought, even in areas traditionally considered unworthy of reflection: Physical Education, for example, and Games.

THE NATIONAL CURRICULUM

You can't write a book in the UK, of course, without writing about National Curriculum subjects. My book is about everything. English is there, as always, throughout. Logic is there. Somebody wrote to me that 'memory and thinking are the same thing', and I knew what they meant, but when I pointed out that you can't remember the future, she was dismissive. She was not dealing with the matter logically; she was not taking language seriously enough. Science is there too. After all, what the Greeks thought of as natural philosophy provides the roots of all subjects. To reflect on, and find out about the planets, or the plants, is a basic philosophic activity, and if they had known about chemistry and physics, and communications, radio, television, cinema, the telephone, mobile phones and the Internet, the Greeks would have treated such knowledge philosophically, too.

There is also Geography and History. How can we think about where we are now, both in time and space, without reflecting on other times, other spaces, other peoples?

A WIDER VIEW OF PHILOSOPHY

It might be said that some ideas in this book are not strictly philosophical. My answer is twofold: first, we need a wider view of what philosophy is compared to the conventional picture of a wild-haired, badly-suited, elderly man wondering about the meaning of life* in an untidy university study; and second, the ways into thinking that I offer will benefit all thinking. Looking at pictures with attention breeds mental precision, and so will looking at nature, buildings, picture books, and the stars. So will playing with words.

---

*I do actually know the meaning of life: but that isn't what philosophy is about, and in any case, I'm saving it for my next book.

One problem with teaching and learning to think is that it can't be displayed on the wall, or demonstrated to parents or in the school assembly. In this competitive age, it is impossible to imagine a secondary school applying for special status by announcing that it is to be an academy for philosophy or thinking. A primary school assembly in which a class demonstrated their ability to reflect by sitting in the Rodin Thinker pose for 15 minutes might win awards for conceptual art, but none for engaging the rest of the school, at least after the first 30 seconds.

Much better to have a specialism in something we can win, like Sport, or put on the wall, like Art, or with which we can demonstrate economic usefulness, like Business Studies. In fact it is the overweening dominance of winning, and economic usefulness, that makes a search for truth all the more important. Philosophy makes us critical in the best sense of that word. To be critical is not to be a fault-finder, but to 'exercise careful judgement'.

I begin with thinking exercises for us as teachers, learning support assistants and other adult workers with children.

NOTE

I have included activities that rely on some basic reading in philosophy for more able children. These activities are boxed. All the children need is a copy of *Sophie's World*, and a good dictionary. They are what are called in today's jargon 'extension activities', but I hope that teachers will use these boxed activities with all the children in mixed-ability pairs.

Thinking ourselves

I am a teacher, and I know that it is illogical, unfair, and doomed to failure to expect children to think unless I think seriously myself. I need to think, first, as a personal habit; second, before I teach; third, while I teach; and fourth, after I've taught. So, for a few pages, here are some exercises for thinking that have helped me.

To start with, an easy one (at least for teachers and learning support assistants who are also parents).

IDEA 1

EVE IN HER GARDEN: A BABY

. . . not in utter nakedness,
But trailing clouds of glory do we come.

William Wordsworth

Reflect on who a baby is. It is all too easy to see her as completely passive, because of her need for vigilant care. We often see her, not as *living* a life, but as *preparing* to live one. In classical paintings of European royal families, the children are not children, but mini-adults. But truly the baby is like Eve in her garden, a learner from the moment of her beginning. She comes into the world ready to be entranced by everything. Look at her fascinated eyes as she is pushed around town in her pram, or as she rests on her father's shoulder, gazing at (literally) Heaven knows what. What are those eyes taking in? One answer, for sure, is: that baby is taking in more than you and I are. She has trailed those clouds into the world, and they inform her every sense experience.

As soon as a baby can talk, she asks questions, and expresses wonderment. It is only later that human beings begin to take things for granted. What can we do to help children to remain fascinated by the world around them? That's a major theme of this book.

Think about what children are learning as they are pushed around in prams or as they are walked around, hands in their parents' hands. Some of the learning can be categorized in National Curriculum terms. They are learning language as they think, listen and talk. They are learning science as they watch branches move in the wind, or waves collapsing on rocks and pebbles. They are learning mathematics as they count all the red cars they see, for example, or all the dogs. They are learning chemistry as they watch a meal being prepared, or, better, as they help to prepare it.

Watch a young child for one day, and note all the evidence of learning. Put it into categories: science, language and so on.

If possible, share findings.

It is instructive to study a baby:

In her pram, as she plays with plastic models strung across within reach of her exploring fingers.

At the edge of an adult's event, a dinner party or whatever. This experience is rare for her, so she studies it hard, until she is tired. We should take time to study her.

I have just spent an evening watching a baby; I'll call him Adam. He is just over a year old. He half-walks, half-crawls around the edges of a drinks party. There is nothing that fails to interest him. Whether he is on the floor, or in his parents' arms, or in mine, he is learning and thinking. On the floor he is interested in the metal handles on a chest of drawers. His fingers and his eyes express that interest.

In his father's arms Adam is interested in what food he can see on the table. In my arms, briefly, but intensely, he is interested in this stranger who shows such interest in him. He smiles briefly, then turns and holds out his arms, communicating with the utmost clarity: 'There is my Daddy. Hand me back, please.'

I have made my notes. Make yours.

WATCHING EVE (AND ADAM)

How do we know the universe began with a big bang, when there weren't any scientists around, not even dinosaur scientists?

5-year-old

Think about 'the things children say'. The phrase crops up everywhere that teachers, learning support assistants and parents meet, and often children are credited with profound and disturbing comments. Everybody has examples: 'I could write a book if I'd collected them . . .'

My son was the last to be ferried about in that Rolls Royce of baby-carriers, a Silver Cross pram. Nowadays, parents and children have buggies. They are Nissans and Skodas by comparison. Anyway, here he is, aged 3, as that pram is being dismembered, wheels detached from the chassis, and stowed away in the loft: 'Are you putting that away for when I'm a baby again?'

Read that sentence again. It took my breath away, still does. What on earth was in his mind? A kind of reincarnation? A notion that he would never die, but come back again as himself? A nostalgia (most likely I think) for the good times, when he was King Baby, with no rivals for his attention?

And here he is again, from the back seat of the family car, aged 5: 'How do we know the universe began with a big bang, when there weren't any scientists around, not even dinosaur scientists?'

Another child:

'What's in your hand, Mummy?'
   'Nothing.'
   'Is the nothing that's in my hand the same as the nothing that's in yours? [pause] Nah, it's a different nothing.'

All children say things like that. The only uniqueness about my son Daniel is that I am his father, and I wrote some of those things down. Get a notebook. Write down some 'things children say', whether they are your own children, or the children you teach.

In a group of colleagues, share some of your stories about things that children have said. Discuss with each other the possible meanings of the children's sayings, and what they might have been trying to express.

Put them in categories, either National Curriculum subjects or, probably more creatively, your own categories. 'Thinking about birth . . . growth . . . death . . . relationships . . . machines . . . nature . . .' We have as a profession got into the habit, through pressure of numbers and administrative duties, of paying less attention than children need.

Listen to children at play, or on a school trip.

I have just walked with children along part of the bank of the River Wear in Durham. Eavesdropping, I heard, within ten minutes:

o 'I am looking into the dark side of you.' (one 10-year-old to another)
o 'When my mum was at the comp, the English teacher used to say when they were naughty, "You brats!"'

Then, me to a misbehaving girl whom I was, with a colleague, trying to befriend and calm: 'Your name, Sarah, means "princess"' (which it does, in Hebrew). Sarah (running away down a bank, over her shoulder): 'You're a liar!'

Reflect: what does this tell us about those children?
Listen to children. Record what they say.

. . . recollected in tranquillity

William Wordsworth

Drop thy still dews of quietness
Till all our strivings cease . . .

John Greenleaf Whittier

Before you consciously help the children to develop their
thinking (you will be doing this un-, sub-, or half-
consciously all the time), think about where, and when,
you did your last thinking.

What was your thinking about?

My last thinking was about an hour ago, after a child
had broken up another child's game of Connect 4 in an
infant class. Among the tears and the bitter reproaches,
I heard myself ask, 'Why did you do that?'

And in relative tranquillity afterwards, I wondered
what I had meant by that question. Had I meant to ask
the child, what was the trigger that made him break up
the game? Or had I meant to ask, what was inside that
made him do it? Reflecting on it, I thought that if it was
the former, what was the point of my question? Would
knowing the answer ('She pushed me', 'She called me a
bad word') help? I thought that probably I meant the
latter. But this, I thought later, was an unanswerable
(and, quite likely, a distressing) question for the child,
who was already disturbed by his tendency to, and his
reputation for, rages. He probably had no idea what
made him lose his rag.

Where were you when you last seriously thought?
How often do we recollect the hurly-burly of school, and
in particular the things we say, in tranquillity?

What were your surroundings? What had you been
doing?

○ reading a newspaper
○ walking (mostly, I don't think as I walk at all. I
  remember)
○ in a place of worship (prayer acts for some as an act
  of self-communion, as well as communion with God)
○ emphatically NOT in a place of worship.

Write down three or four settings where thinking feels impossible:

○ in a football crowd
○ in a pub
○ when seriously stressed or depressed
○ when driving.

Our best conditions for thinking as adults should be replicated as much as possible in the school where we teach thinking. This needs a school policy, facing up to challenges such as 'Is the classroom ever quiet?'; 'How can we make it quieter?'; 'Have children anywhere to go during playtimes and lunchtimes to be quiet?'; 'Is time for serious thought ever provided in assembly?'; 'Where can they find tranquillity?'

Is there any sense in which the word 'skill' is wrong for thinking?

It has a noble etymology. It originally denoted the mind's ability to make distinctions. But today it is a much reduced word. We customarily use it when we are thinking about activities that are measurable. It is easy to measure a learner-swimmer's or a learner-cyclist's progress, or a child's trudging through a reading scheme. Is 'thinking' as easily measurable?

Make two lists: of activities that are measurable, and that therefore suit the word 'skill'; and other activities, such as 'thinking', 'dreaming', 'wondering', 'aspiring' or 'praying' that, therefore, don't. Can you imagine the first learning objective, or target, in a list of prayer skills? 'Places hands accurately together . . .'

The title of this book was originally *100 Ideas for Teaching Thinking Skills in the Primary School*. What word would you put in the place of '*thinking skills*'? Attitudes? I would have liked to introduce the word 'philosophy' here.

THE WORD 'SKILLS'

IDEA

8

THINK

Do some thinking. Read an editorial or a letter in the *Guardian, Independent, The Times* or the *Daily Telegraph* and think hard. Then make some notes for the case against the argument that the paper is making. Watch out for slippery words and phrases, such as 'We find . . .' (who is this 'we'?) and 'It will be seen that', (by whom will be seen that?). A local politician I once knew was fond of introducing a point about which there was disagreement with 'Fairly obviously . . .' when it wasn't obvious at all. It was an empty piece of rhetoric to try to disarm his opponents.

There was a letter in the *Guardian* (26 July 2007) defending the foundation of a call centre in a secondary school to train young people in selling mobile phones. The correspondent wrote that the perception of '. . . the satanic mills type of call centre is *in many cases* wrong'. For anyone who thinks critically, the phrase I have italicized gives the argument away. So the rest *are* like satanic mills?

There is a difference between being cynical about political argument ('Well, he would say that, wouldn't he?') and being critical. The former is easy to do, and little use. The second is harder, and requires thought.

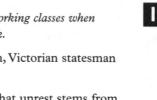
We are more frightened of the working classes when they think than when they drink.

Viscount Groschen, Victorian statesman

Can this be true?

The conventional wisdom is that unrest stems from drinking, but this argument suggests that while cheap gin in Victorian London may have led to fighting, domestic violence and the like, it also kept the working classes where the authorities wanted them: at the bottom of the heap. They were, therefore, less likely to band together in effective political movements agitating for reform. The fact that they were often dead drunk may have been regrettable, but it had two advantages: the upper and middle classes could feel morally superior, and it made for a quieter life for them.

Similarly, the Roman authorities thought that the lower classes could be kept quiet as long as they were given their 'bread and circuses'. They knew that a food shortage would endanger the safety of the emperors and the aristocracy, while food and entertainment in abundance would lead to security for them.

Is it in any authority's interest for us to think? If it is, why are our professional lives crowded with obstacles: planning meetings, evaluation meetings . . . meetings about anything except what makes us human, what requires genuine thinking?

Are similar obstacles placed in the way of children when they think? Can they think as they approach SATs week, for example? Or as they are told, when writing a story, 'I want this finished before lunchtime'?

What obstacles can you think of that are in the way both of your thinking and their thinking? Young teachers with English degrees invariably tell me that they have no time to read. So is it likely that they have time to think?

DO 'THEY' WANT US TO THINK?

11

. . . education . . . rendered the working classes unfitted for good servants and labourers.

Queen Victoria

Discuss: What differences and similarities are there between that attitude to education and ours today?

Is it education's purpose to staff tomorrow's service industries (the modern equivalent of good servants and labourers), or to offer individuals 'abundant life'? The former view, which sociologists call functionalism, is exemplified in the news (referred to in Idea 8) that a secondary school in the UK has set up an 'on-site call centre where students can practise selling mobile phones' (*Guardian* 23 July 2007).

Lady Bracknell, in Oscar Wilde's play *The Importance of Being Earnest*, says that

Fortunately, in England at any rate, education has no effect whatsoever. If it did, it would prove a serious danger to the upper classes, and probably lead to acts of violence in Grosvenor Square.

Again, discuss. This is, of course, a joke. But Wilde, as in all the best jokes, is making a serious point.

'ACTS OF VIOLENCE IN GROSVENOR SQUARE'

According to the American educationist Howard Gardner, we don't have just the two intelligences that he calls 'linguistic' and 'logical-mathematic': we have seven. The others are (in his terms) 'personal', 'social', 'artistic', 'physical', and 'spiritual/moral'. In schools, he suggests, we concentrate on the first two, and neglect the others.

Individually and in a group, identify ways in which the school's practice in these five supposed neglected areas could be improved. For example:

PERSONAL AND SOCIAL
What work do we do with children that might help them to make and sustain peace with other children? I mean work that is positive, and not just reacting to sudden violence on the playground, or to national disasters (see Ideas 81 and 82).

ARTISTIC
What work do we do with children that might help them to understand works of art and architecture, and to see what those works do to help us understand the human world? (See Ideas 55–58.)

PHYSICAL
What work do we do with children that might help them understand the value of physical education and games? (See Ideas 66–68.)

SPIRITUAL/MORAL
What work do we do with children that might help them understand different perspectives, from the atheistic to the avowedly religious, to understand how to live the good life? (Throughout.)

Name some situations when it is right to lie. For example, a family harbouring a Jewish family in Nazi Germany would lie to a Gestapo officer who asked, 'Is there anyone in your attic/cellar?'

Recently there was a news story that told how a woman had lied about her premature child's birthdate, because if the doctors had known her correct age the child wouldn't have received the necessary health care.

Those are both serious situations about life and death, of course. What about trivial situations? What about when someone asks you what you think of their new shirt or their new dress when both are ill-fitting, the wrong colours and vulgar? Do you lie or tell the truth?

What was the last 'white lie' that you told?

One lie that I feel strongly about is a common reply to 'Fancy a pint Thursday?' and it goes, 'Yeah, I'd love to, not sure if I can, I'll give you a ring about six on Thursday and let you know', which means 'Yeah, sure, unless I get a better offer'.

Make a statement, on your own, about the purpose of education, or why you are a teacher. Share these statements in groups.

Think about the following statements, all of which I have been offered recently in responses to a questionnaire:

○ To enable children to take their place in a capitalist society
○ To help children inherit their traditions
○ To help children to critique the traditional ways of life in their society
○ To help children to fulfil their potential
○ To help children to use their inherent creativity

Work out the ideologies behind these statements. Look at them. Note the keywords, which are, according to me (by all means find others): 'capitalist', 'traditions' (and 'traditional'), 'inherit', 'critique', 'potential' and 'creativity'.

Identify the keywords in your own statements. Work out the ideologies behind them. For example, 'capitalist' is easy to see in political terms. But so are 'traditions' and 'creativity'.

In a group, each class teacher, special educational needs coordinator, headteacher, and learning support assistant prepares a note about one child's behaviour in school: his or her work, play, social behaviour, emotional presentation, learning styles (impetuous, thoughtful), personality (quiet, noisy, introspective), and so on – everything except test results. Everyone reads the notes about the child, and the others discuss those notes.

When discussing the notes, useful comments and questions are:

○ Give us the evidence for that.
○ Why do you say that?
○ What do you mean by that?

It is important to challenge comments that seem obvious, but that may only seem so because they have been repeated so often.

Bear in mind that there are times when we are doing nothing, or doing something relatively inconsequential – shaving, ironing, walking the dog, going to sleep, waking up, lying in the bath – and thoughts come to us unbidden. Serious writers always carry a notebook and serious artists always carry a sketchbook. We should follow their example.

Start a notebook, and record random thoughts. To prevent it becoming precious and pretentious, this book should also be used for trivia like shopping lists, and to-do lists.

There are many games to help children think, and many of them are collected in Robert Fisher's *Games for Thinking*. Get hold of this book, and discuss it. An early example is the Dictionary Race, where you give children words, and they have to race to find definitions. I am sure games like this can be useful, but I am troubled by the competitive element. I remember a remark of T. S. Eliot: 'in poetry, there is no competition . . .' And in philosophy? Is competition an element in thinking? Discuss . . .

Other books by Fisher include *Poems, Stories, Games* and *Values for Thinking*, all published by Nash Pollock.

Thinking in the classroom

Better get into the classroom. The children wait there, with a serious library of knowledge already garnered both joyfully and painfully, in their minds and hearts. What can we teach them? And what can they teach us? Let's not reduce the history of Ancient Egypt to a collage of Tutankhamun's tomb, or Henry VIII's reign to a wall of dead, tissue paper images of discarded queens. Let's help the children to think.

GROUND RULES FOR TALKING

Cogito, ergo sum, as the seventeenth-century French philosopher René Descartes famously wrote. I think, therefore I am.

But we also need to *talk* about our thinking. The children should help in the building of a framework that will enable talk, first because building that framework entails thinking, and second because each child's thinking will not be honoured in the subsequent discussion unless the talk is fair, and they have to make sure it's fair on their terms as well as yours. Indeed, after a few minutes, they should take this exercise over.

You might begin by saying: It is everyone's responsibility to make sure that there is thinking time before talk begins. There is not enough silence or, in Wordsworth's word, tranquillity, in many primary schools. And often what silence exists is of the low level kind that follows the instructions to 'Be quiet while I do the register' or to 'Be quiet so I hear myself think'. The latter instruction includes a grain of truth. We do, indeed, need quietness to help us think. But it is not usually what the speaker means.

You can follow this first statement with:

o It is everyone's responsibility to make sure all have opportunities to speak.
o It is everyone's responsibility to be patient. Some express ideas tentatively, and many who express them quickly put them badly.
o Everyone should understand that you, the teacher, don't know everything. Some teachers allow the children to see their ignorance and uncertainty about certain subjects. In any case, the teacher should aim to be 'a neutral chair'.

You might also suggest that the group should establish the use of a conch, or something like it: in *The Lord of the Flies* by William Golding, a group of boys, shipwrecked on a remote island, try to form a parliament. One rule is that only the boy holding a conch shell may speak. Anything will do as a substitute for a conch – a class photograph, a small globe, or a soft toy.

The group should also phase out 'hands up!'

Ask the children if they have any more suggestions. And tell them: all these rules, prominently and readably displayed at eye-level in the classroom, must be observed during the following sessions. Ask them to note how the words 'everyone's responsibility' and 'group' re-occur.

Know then thyself, presume not God to scan,
The proper study of mankind is man.

Alexander Pope

A MAP OF A MIND

Not all the activities in this book require talking. This one doesn't.

There is a problem in seeking and gaining self-knowledge. Almost everyone would agree that it is an indispensable condition of the good, reflective life. But as a novelist once said on a radio broadcast: 'Self-knowledge is all very well as long as you're a good chap.' The great German poet Johann Wolfgang von Goethe put it more elegantly: 'I do not know myself, and God forbid that I should.' Nevertheless, I am going to proceed as though self-knowledge is necessary to our understanding.

Ask the children to draw a map of their minds. It doesn't need to be accurate, or well drawn. But it must be truthful. Tell them, 'Put in your feelings, joys, fear, memories, thoughts . . . Give them shapes or colours that you think suit them.' The drawing can be representational, or abstract.

Ask them to make the most important things in their minds either the biggest part of the drawings, or else to put them in the position they think right for the most important thing. Prompt them by asking: Where will you put the things that make you happy? And where will you put the things that make you sad?

Show them how, in atlases or on globes, different parts of the earth are marked in different ways. Tell them that, as maps in atlases have words on them to make things clearer, so their mind maps should have words. These can be whole sentences, or merely labels.

Ask them to reflect on what they have drawn and written.

This is a way of looking inside oneself. It stems from a poem by Kit Wright ('The Magic Box', the last poem in his collection *Cat Among the Pigeons*), but like many other jobbing poets, I have developed it in my own way.

Ask the children to reflect on, and then write down, answers to the following questions. I have interleaved my questions with one 9-year-old's answers.

There's a box in your head. It's made of the materials that are most beautiful to you. They need not be things you can touch (it is best if some of the children offer abstract nouns, as in the example given here). What are those materials?

> *My box is made of rainbows, my mother's kisses, and the sound of flute music.*

Your box opens, and it opens like you. How does it open?

> *It opens gently, like this* [she opened her fingers like a flower opening] *without a sound.*

Inside is your most treasured possession. What is it?

> *Inside it is a necklace my Nan brought back from Greece for me. She's dead now.*

Inside it is an impossible thing that is beautiful . . .

> *There is peace in the world, and nobody is hungry.*

Inside your box are three memories. What are they?

> *I remember the day in France when I got lost in a supermarket. I remember my first piano lesson. I remember my Nan's smile.*

Your box closes. How does it feel now that it is closed?

> *I am glad all my things are safe.*

IDEA

20

Read out the following statement by Sarah, a 10-year-old girl. I had given her a word frame, 'I am a . . .' and asked her to complete it with words summing up an ambition or a dream. This second clause must have two parts: she came up with *I am a skilled pop-singer/with a pure heart.* (In other words, the noun 'pop-singer' wasn't enough. She needed a phrase beginning 'with a . . . ' or 'and I . . . '.)

Ask the children to do the same, but discourage 'pop-singer': 'That is Sarah's beginning. You can't have it. You must invent your own.' Warning: 'I am a footballer' rarely goes anywhere interesting.

Then, get the children to write sentences with these frames. They don't have to have two parts now, but they must be as comprehensive as they can make them. I have put Sarah's answers in italics:

I always believe that
My family are watching over me.

I sometimes believe that
My family will never die.

I cry when
I reach the pure centre of myself when I sing.

I want
To be so great that evil spirits never come.

I understand
What energy children feel when they sing.

Other writing frames are: 'I worry about . . .'; 'I sometimes believe that . . .'; 'I rejoice when . . .'; 'I laugh when . . .'; 'When I think of heaven, I think of . . .'; 'I wonder if . . .'; 'I pray that/for . . .', and 'I understand that . . .'

A few moments' thought will uncover other writing frames that will enrich this exercise.

SHARING THOUGHTS

Some children will want to be quiet, even secretive, about what they have written. But most of them want – need even – to share it.

Get the children to share, if they want to, their box writing, their 'I'm a pop-singer . . .' writing, and their mind maps with each other in a small group. Always tell them that they may have written sentences that they want, or need, to keep secret, and that it is important that they do so.

Then ask the children: Who would like to read their box writing to the rest of the class? Some will, and some of those children who stand up will have written distressing things, often about death. It is important that they are given the floor, that they are given a respectful silence, and that there is a pause afterwards while the rest of those present digest what the child has said.

If they have mentioned truly distressing incidents in their lives, I always say, 'That isn't just good writing, it is brave writing', and I explain that much of the best writing requires courage, and we give them a round of applause. The reaction of the rest of the class is always respectful.

You go not till I set you up a glass
Where you may see the inmost part of you . . .

Hamlet

Have some mirrors available. Begin by asking the children about things they see when they look in them – brown eyes, red hair, freckles etc. I often ask the children to draw their faces carefully at this point: line drawings with no colour. 'Can I colour it in?' betrays a lack in a child's art education. Colour is more than decoration, and in these drawings will only obscure, rather than clarify, meaning.

Then quote those lines from Hamlet, and ask the children (making it clear that this is not about physical things like liver, lungs, muscles and bones): What would you see inside your heart, or your soul, if you could hold a mirror up to them?

Here are some sentences that children have written:

○ In my heart are libraries for knowledge and as I grow the libraries get bigger.
○ You'd see my dark side . . . blue and black with a flash of red for life. You'd see my fears, life is my biggest fear. I'm small, the world's big . . .

Ask the children to write their sentences on their drawings. The result should be a coherent work of art in two media – line drawing and words. They could find ways of writing sentences that enhance the final product.

'THE INMOST PART'

AND IT WAS STILL HOT

After all that introspection, here is something more outward-looking.

Picture books enchant children when they are young. Although these books are almost all written for 5- to 7-year-olds, they make older children think and, in fact, still enchant them. My experience suggests that we underuse them in Years 4, 5 and 6. We should bring them into Key Stage Two classrooms for three reasons. First, they are good books, written with both a sense of the rhythm of children's thoughts and speech, and also with sensitivity towards their loves and hates. Second, they bring back happy memories for nearly all children. And third, they are absorbing books for adults, and this comes across when you read them. If anyone sees an 11-year-old re-reading one of these books and says (as some people do) that their son or daughter is beyond that, they are not thinking about books, but about the mechanics of phonics, which is a different matter.

I have read *Where the Wild Things Are* by Maurice Sendak, sometimes to children, and sometimes to myself, dozens of times, and still love it. Here are some suggested discussion triggers for *Where the Wild Things Are*:

o Find some words to describe how Max has been behaving.
o What might make you behave like that?
o How did Max get to the land where the Wild Things are?
o Apart from their land, where else are the Wild Things?
o Are they perhaps in his head? (Some children will, if you give them time, suggest this.)
o Do you ever have Wild Things in your head?
o If so, what kind of things do they do?
o What makes you think that Max's mother and father love him?

Other recommended books are:

o *Not Now Bernard* by David McKie. This book examines the problems felt by a child who feels neglected by his well-meaning parents.
o *Princess Smartypants* by Babette Cole. This book brings to the fore issues about sexual roles.

○ *Amazing Grace* by Mary Hoffman. This book addresses questions about racial pride and about racist feelings. It will move any class, of whatever age, to thought. It still moves me to tears.

When I read these books to older children, I leave long silences, so that they can think. In fact, I need to think, too.

I said at the beginning of this idea that it was more 'outward-looking' than the ones that went before it. And it is. But note that looking at good books inevitably leads to self-examination.

EMPIRICAL AND RATIONAL

Frogs and fish and anemones and poppies

Aristotle

'Rational', 'empirical'. Ask the children to find these words in a grown-up dictionary. To be rational (from the Latin, '*ratio*', reason) is to rely on reason. On the other hand, to be empirical (from the Greek word for experience) is to rely on the senses. The next nine sessions are examples of stimuli to empirical thinking.

Ask the children who have explored the meanings of these words to look at page 89 of *Sophie's World*, and to answer the question: Was Plato a rationalist or an empiricist? And Aristotle? The key words are: 'the eternal world of ideas' (Plato) and 'frogs and fish and anemones and poppies' (Aristotle).

Tell them, we are now going to be empirical, and examine 'frogs and fish and anemones and poppies'. In other words we are going to try to understand aspects of the world through our senses. Plato's 'eternal world of ideas' will have to wait for another time . . .

The poet W.H. Auden called the senses 'the precious five'. They are necessary to any thinking that isn't aiming to be entirely theoretical – that is, rationalist. You can be theoretical, of course, but children will think more clearly, and become better philosophers, if they take their evidence from their experiences. This means being intensive users of their senses.

Ask the children to close and cover their eyes with their hands. What can they hear? Ask the children to listen for sounds.

What can they hear:

o Inside their own body?
o In the room?
o Outside the room, but inside the building?
o Outside the building?

Always remember that their hearing is almost certainly more acute than yours. They may hear things that you can't. Give them the benefit of the doubt.

Ask them to write down what they have heard, and then to talk about it.

Silence is when you hear things

John Cotton

We often hear vaguely without truly listening, and we often look vaguely without truly seeing. A homely example: I have often looked for the kitchen scissors, when they are under my nose, without seeing them.

Ask the children to listen with care. Right now, on a Sunday morning at 7a.m., I can hear a wood pigeon, another higher-voiced bird that I can't identify, the traffic's low moan a hundred yards away, and the ring on my right hand knocking on the table as I write.

Ask the children to listen:

○ In the classroom
○ In a place of worship
○ In the woods, or the fields, or by the seaside, or beside a road.

What would they hear if they could hear things they normally can't hear? Use this poem by John Cotton:

LISTEN

Silence is when you hear things.
Listen:
The breathing of bees,
A moth's footfall,
Or the mist easing its way
Across the field,
The light shifting at dawn
Or the stars clicking into place
At evening.

We should look at something until it hurts

William Blake

The poet George Tardios wrote that 'the world is troubled with a lack of looking' (quoted in Jill Pirrie's book about writing poetry, *On Common Ground*, Hodder and Stoughton 1987).

I was teaching a class to write 'snapshot poems'. These poems require them to capture the objects they are looking at in three or four lines.

One boy couldn't start. He'd written his name at the top of his paper, and nothing else. I asked him to look at the wall of a house. 'What can you see on that wall?' 'Bricks.' 'Anything else?' 'Concrete.' (He meant mortar, I suppose.)

No one had taught him to see the sunlight on the bricks, that brightened some of them, and left others in the dark, or the sway of the branches' shadows as the branches were being driven by the strong wind. His schooling had let him down. He could only see his name, barren at the top of his paper, and, when pressed, bricks and mortar.

This was 'a lack of looking', indeed. He had never looked at anything, let alone, as William Blake said we should, 'until it hurts'.

Ask the children to stand on the field or playground, and cover their ears, and look for things that are quite still. Then ask them:

○ to look at things that move, but are rooted
○ to look at things that move freely
○ to think of words that describe the movement of things in the last two groups.

These little poems provoke, in the making of them, intense looking and hearing.

On the day after the children have looked 'until it hurts' at branches, grass and trees, or even better immediately after they have looked at those things, ask them to take word-snapshots of what they've been looking at. These word-snapshots will take the shape of little poems.

Here are two snapshot poems, one for Spring, and one for Winter. They only involve sight:

All down the grass verges
bridesmaids in their pink and white
and pale green dresses.

Icing on earth's cake –
underneath, such rich fruit
waiting for a birth.

(FS)

Ask the children to write snapshot poems, and to read them to each other in groups; thus first using sight, and then, hearing.

Ovid (43 BC–AD 17)

Most of the books that I've seen on 'thinking skills' pay no attention to the natural world. This is odd, because, as I have written earlier, the earliest western philosophers, the Greeks who came before the great trio, Plato, Socrates and Aristotle, who provide the basis for western philosophy, were obsessed with natural philosophy.

They were especially interested in change. They had noticed that water changed into ice, for example, and they'd thought about it; that colours changed as the seasons passed; that animals grew from small and helpless, to gawky, to smooth and efficient. 'How do things change from one into another?' they wondered. Change fascinated them, as it should us.

But although many of us have learned, if that is the right word, to take change for granted, nature constantly transforms itself. Leaves wither and drop. Snow falls, hardens into ice and thaws. New leaves reappear. Blossoms, whether we notice or not, flourish. Summer arrives, and we notice that . . .

'Dripping water', as the Roman poet Ovid noticed, 'hollows out a stone'. And he kept watching.

Take the children out once more. Ask them to look at things changing as they watch: cloud shapes, leaf and branch movements, movements in the tops of trees, grass in the wind. Then ask them to record the changes that they have noted, and finally, in groups, to share what they have seen.

IDEA 30

CHANGE GOES ON . .

Ask the children: How does nature change over seasons? Get them to keep a log about the appearance of the school site over a school year, prompting them with suggestions about leaves, trees, flowers, grass and clouds.

Then ask: What human-made things have changed this place? There will be new buildings, for example, extensions, and new roads. Trees are cut down.

Finally, what about changes in our own appearances? The children should record their height, for example, in September, and then at monthly intervals through the school year.

Change and decay in all around I see

H.F. Lyte 'Abide with me'

Ask the children to reflect on what the same site may have looked like a hundred years ago. Get them to do research in local museums and on websites. In every town, there are, somewhere, photographic records of towns as they were in Victorian times up to the present. You can often find cheap books with titles like *Ipswich* (my town) *in Victorian Times*, or *Ipswich Between the Wars* in remainder shops. The Works chain of cheap bookshops is an under-used resource for schools for local history.

Ask the children: Can you imagine what this scene that you watch now will look like in a hundred years? What technological changes are likely to change the towns we live in now? Introduce ideas about global warming. Explain that this is natural philosophy. Introduce ideas, too, about the decline of industry, and the growth of other ways of doing business: the service industries.

AND ON

A hedgehog scuttles furtively over the lawn

Thomas Hardy, 'Afterwards'

Ask the children to watch the behaviour of animals, both in the classroom and at home. Ask them to make notes.

Some animals keep themselves clean. Others don't, and humans have to wash them. Ask them to write an account of bathing the dog, or of watching a cat licking its fur. Does a hamster keep itself clean? A rabbit?

How does each animal eat and drink? Ask them to watch a pet drinking. Focus on the animal's tongue.

For some animals, sight is the primary sense. For others, it is smell. Can they judge, from the animal's behaviour, which is the primary sense of a particular animal in a particular situation?

Ask the children if their cats can recognize themselves in a mirror. My cat, Stanley, can't. Is this because he is dim? He is, but that isn't the reason. He needs the sense of smell as much as I need the senses of sight and hearing. Or is it that the notion of an image, so familiar to me, is as foreign to him as his sly hunting life at the fringes of my garden is to me?

Have them write adjectives describing each animal's movement – not just the movement in their legs, but in their noses as they sense food, in their eyes as they watch prey. Ask the children to note how still a cat's eyes are when they see or smell something they need, and are intent on getting it.

*He who cannot draw on three thousand years'
experience is living from hand to mouth.*

Goethe

Write those words up, or give them out on sheets
to a small group of children.

Ask: What does Goethe mean about 3,000
years? He is talking about all the important
thinking that has gone on in the world since over a
thousand years before the birth of Christ.

Ask some of the children to look at *Sophie's
World*, pp 29–32 to explore more of what the
Ancient Greeks thought about change. Ask them
to find out what Parmenides thought: his reason
told him that nothing could change; therefore,
when he perceived change through his senses,
those senses had to be wrong.

And what about Heraclitus? His senses told
him that everything changes, and he trusted his
senses.

Is this of any use to us?

I think it is. What Goethe means is that it is not
enough to rely on the knowledge of our own time
or even, worse, the knowledge of our own culture.

MORE FROM SOPHIE'S WORLD

Who are you? . . . Where does the world come from?

Jostein Gaarder, *Sophie's World*

Ask the children to look up, in the index to *Sophie's World*: 'Oracle at Delphi, The.' What was it? What was its great message? Can they think of ways to obey that command?

A very big question is printed twice in italics on p 4: WHO ARE YOU? Ask them to write an answer to that question.

Ask the children to define themselves, in as many ways as possible, from 'I am a dancer/singer/actor/footballer/gymnast' through to 'I am a supporter of Ipswich Town/Norwich City' and 'I am a believer in chance' and 'I am a person who has black moods sometimes' or 'I am a believer/non-believer in God'.

There's another big question at the bottom of p 6: WHERE DOES THE WORLD COME FROM? Ask the children to think about that. Then they should write notes on their thinking. And then, remembering their responsibilities to each other (see Idea 17), they should discuss what they have written.

Let us eat, drink and be merry

St Luke 15:23

I like white bread
and almost anything fried
but my mum's in a healthy eating phase
and though I've really tried

to show that what's, well, good
isn't always good *for you*
she buys granary loaves, and lentils, and split peas
and makes healthy vegetable stew.

(FS)

This lesson should be linked to the lessons, which are everywhere now, about eating that doesn't harm us, and that, more positively, does us good. The recent emphasis on healthy food should go along with an emphasis on food that is good in other ways: it tastes interesting, it is fresh, and it is less destructive to the environment than some food is (more of this in Idea 63).

Ask the children: What is food for?

o To be enjoyed, first in the cooking of it, and second, in the eating of it.
o To keep us healthy, and to prolong our lives.

We need a balance between enjoyment and keeping us alive, of course. Food that is only pleasurable won't help us live well. But food that is merely healthy may be boring.

Ask the children to make three lists: what tastes good to them, and what tastes bad, and what is just . . . boring. Now ask them, using the information they will already have about healthy eating, to list what is good for you, what is bad, and what is somewhere in the middle. Then ask them to write a recipe for a meal that gets the balance right: healthy, tasty, something naughty . . .

Ask them: Who cooks in your house? Who *should* cook in your house?

Read this poem to the children

QUIET

Once there was quiet in the valley,
We could hear the slow thoughts of mountains,
The breathing of slow hills
And at evening the dark forest trees listening
*   to the silence.*
Then came traffic
And it was never the same.
The earth stopped hearing
And the still voices were drowned.
Though sometimes in the small hours
The quiet will pay its sly secret visits
From where it waits.

(John Cotton)

Ask the children to start conversations with relatives and friends about the world and our treatment of it; to read newspapers; to watch television and listen to radio; and to Google topics like 'conservation of forests'.

Ask them to collect examples of the way the earth is changing, and to bring them in tomorrow. These examples could include:

o Depletion of fuel stocks
o Weather changes, both in the UK and abroad
o Loss of animal species
o Loss of forests.

What can *we* do about these issues? What, for example, do *we* use that contributes, for example, to the loss of fuel stocks?

Ask the children if they can find out about any methods of transport that are fairer to the environment. Then suggest: But – many of us want to fly when and where we want, and many of us want to be able to drive where we want.

Like so many difficult problems, there is a balance to be struck, between personal freedom and the preservation of the environment.

Next day, collect the examples that children have brought in. Explore the issues that have arisen. Ask what we can do about them:

o Individually
o As families
o As members of a school.

Then, ask them: Is *all* the change in the world for the worse? That's what we might think, reading John Cotton's poem and the papers and watching television. Can they think of any changes that are for the good?

THINKING ABOUT THE WORLD AGAIN

He was a man who used to notice such things

Thomas Hardy, 'Afterwards'

That's a line from a poem by Thomas Hardy that I've already quoted (Idea 32). It's what he hoped people would say of him after he'd died. He meant things in nature: 'the dewfall-hawk . . . crossing the shades', 'the hedgehog scuttles furtively over the lawn', and the way 'a crossing breeze cuts a pause' in a bell's 'outrollings'.

Take the children for a walk. The aim – or the objective, or the target – is to notice things in nature that they have never noticed before: the shape of a leaf, or its resemblance to something else, for example. The word 'like' is useful here, in simile-inducing mode: the leaf 'looks like', or the leaf 'resembles', or the leaf 'reminds me of . . .'.

Do the same with: an animal's behaviour (the way some birds walk, and some hop, for example); the movement of clouds; and the feel of the bark of a tree. Back in the classroom, ask the children to make a list of what they have noticed for the first time. Both the watching and the listing will involve serious thought. Ask them to share what they noticed for the first time.

It's not only in nature that things change. Take the children on an urban walk. Again, ask them to look for things that they haven't noticed before. Even in their lifetimes, a shop will have changed from one business to another, or a shop will have become empty, or a building will have been demolished, and another put up in its place.

Ask the children to watch for changes happening now. In my town at the moment, as in many, there is much demolition going on, and much building, mostly blocks of flats.

Ask the children to research building changes. They might write to local councils and to newspapers, by post and by email.

(For more on looking at towns, see Idea 58.)

NOTICING THINGS IN TOWN

Ask the children to cover their faces with some translucent material: net curtains, for example.

Ask them: Does the world look the same as it did before? No. It looks the same, but grey. That is what it is to be rational: we have something across the front of our mind that encourages us to see the world in a certain way, like that net curtain.

We all have some net curtains across the front of our minds:

o The way we were brought up, and how we remember our growing up
o What our parents taught us, and how we remember that, and think about it, and adapt it
o What priests, ministers, imams, and rabbis taught us at church, or in the mosque, or in the synagogue, or that we interpret for ourselves.

But above all, we have our careful thinking about why something happens. This is thinking that we do without the benefit of our senses. We know, for example, what the sun and the moon do, without the experience of 'our precious five'.

The net curtain is not a bad thing: we could not live without rational thought. Empiricist thinkers, on the other hand, believe that we learn through the senses.

Note that all empiricists have net curtains, too! They are sometimes rationalist. And that all rationalists take on information every day through their senses. They are empiricist, too.

Sit on a potato pan, Otis

Palindromic sentence. Anon

If all that was a bit heavy, relax with some word games.

Tell the children that the name 'Hannah' is a palindrome. Ask them to find out what 'palindrome' means. Now ask them to find some three-letter palindromes, for example: Bob, Ada, Dad, Mum, did, dud, gag, gig, Nan, Oho!, pop, tot, tit. There aren't too many place name palindromes: the name of the town Eye in Suffolk is one.

Now ask them to find some four-letter ones: Toot, noon, peep, Anna. And some five-letter ones: level, civic, refer.

Ask the children to find, in an encyclopaedia, or by Googling, a sentence that is a palindrome. Here are three famous ones:

○ Able was I ere I saw Elba.
○ Sit on a potato pan, Otis.
○ A man, a plan, a canal, Panama.

PALINDROMES

45

IDEA
42

ISOGRAMS

Daniel and I go to Orkney this year

A sentence made entirely of isogrammatic words.

Tell the children: Four of those palindromes in Idea 41 are also isograms: Anna, toot, noon and peep. Can they guess what an isogram is?

It is a word in which each letter appears a certain number of times. In these words, it's twice, so they are called 'second-order isograms'.

A first-order isogram is a word where each letter appears once. There are thousands, probably millions of them. Ask them to find some. My Christian name is one: Fred. My surname is, too: Sedgwick. That's how common they are. Here are some more: first, the, an, dream, groan, frame, desk, love, death. If you are broad-minded enough, tell them there is a rude word that is an isogram (fart). Can they think of a one-letter isogram? There are two: 'a' and 'I'.

Ask the children to go through the class's names, and put them in two groups: isograms on the left, non-isograms on the right. Bethany will be on the same side with Mark, Colin, Joginder, Amrit, Gulab, Meg, and Morag. But Jimmy, Mohammed, David, Christopher and Ravendeep will be on the other side.

Ask them to find the longest first-order isogram they can. If your school is in Worcestershire, about three miles east of Evesham and about eight miles north-east of Tewkesbury, you live in the longest first-order isogrammatic place in Britain.*

How many of the names of the months are first-order isograms? It's five, according to me. And of the days of the week? Once more, I make it five.

Now ask them to find some second-order isograms.

(For this Idea, I acknowledge David Crystal, the linguist, and an article of his in the *Guardian* on 19 May 2007.)

---

*The longest first-order isogrammatic placename in Britain is, according to David Crystal, Bricklehampton. Other isograms are: Edinburgh, Durham, Malvern, and Dublin.

Explain to the children that an anagram is a word whose letters, when put in a different order, make up another word.

In these sentences, the words or phrases 'mixed' 'jumbled' and 'all over the place' (or something similar) tell you that you have an anagram to solve: they 'signal' an anagram. The words that make up the anagram are 'anagram fodder'. For example, in the first clue, 'carthorse' makes up the anagram fodder and 'mixed' signals the anagram. There is also another part of the clue, the definition, which in this case is 'makes music'. Scrabble tiles are a great help in solving anagrams.

○ Mixed carthorse makes music. (9 letters)
○ I am a weakish speller jumbled, but I wrote great plays. (7,11)
   'I am a weakish speller' is the anagram fodder, 'jumbled' signals that there is an anagram, and 'I wrote great plays' is the definition.
○ Trophy rater got mixed up at Hogwarts. (5,6)
○ And moan all over the place, famous singer. (7)
○ Spies chop messily for David's wife. (4,5)
○ In wimp's gloom messed up I do a length. (8,4)
○ Mercy! Hate mixed – for Miss or Sir. (2,7)★

If they have trouble with these, add 'with conductor' to the first, 'famous for two starcrossed lovers' for the second, 'wears round glasses' for the third, 'begins with M' for the fourth, 'David plays football' for the fifth and 'splash!' for the sixth. They don't need a clue for the last, I think.

That's enough fooling. We must go back to the serious business of philosophy.

Answers: orchestra, William Shakespeare, Harry Potter, Madonna, Posh Spice, swimming pool, my teacher.

THINKING ABOUT THINKING

Does this sound like navel-gazing? In fact, it's a part of philosophy that many thinkers deem important. What do we do when we think? It's not as simple as many of us suppose.

Put the following sentences on display:

o 'I think I need a new pair of trainers'
o 'I think I'll have the fiorentina pizza'
o 'I think I fancy some chips'
o 'I think that the moon is made of green cheese'
o 'I think that [any name here] is the best singer/footballer in the world . . .'
o 'I think that God is a kind of universal goodness that we can't understand . . .'

Ask the children: Does the word 'think' mean the same in each sentence?

Then ask them to complete sentences like this:

o 'When I think of peace, I think of . . .'
o 'When I think of love, I think of . . .'
o 'When I think of God/Allah, I think of . . .'
o 'When I think of my future, I think of . . . '

Tell the children that it seems that thinking is more than 'I think I fancy some chips'. Discuss.

This session, and the next few, are about thinking about love. 'Think', as we have seen, can mean different things. So can 'love'. Love is the big word in the Bible and in nearly all popular culture.

Give the children these sentences (and, even better, some you can think of):

- I love chips
- I love my mum (sister, dad, brother, auntie, uncle, grandfather, grandmother)
- I love my football team (or my favourite pop group)
- I love the way my cat cleans himself
- I will love my boyfriend/girlfriend
- I will love my husband/wife
- I love the sky at night
- I love Paris in the springtime
- I love the way you wrinkle your nose
- I love God.

Ask them to look at the word 'love' in all those sentences: does 'love' always mean the same thing? Obviously, it doesn't. For example, one probably wouldn't cry (though one might!) if there were no chips for a week, but one might very well cry if one couldn't see Mum, or Dad, or a sister or brother for a week. One might cry, too, if one's football team lost – but not, I hope, for long.

Here is a poem by Gareth:

A TREE CLIMBER TO HIS MOTHER
You are
the safety net
under every branch
I stand on.

Ask the children to think hard about someone they love.
It is best to restrict them to adults. Otherwise, this
session could turn soppy and embarrassing. Then ask
them to think about a subject or an area of knowledge in
which they are strong: ballet, football, music, garden,
flowers, geography etc. Ask them to combine their love
with that subject, as Gareth has done.

Here are some examples by children. The first was
addressed to a father:

You are the goal against United
And the screams of Anfield.
I run through the tunnel and touch you for luck . . .

This one was addressed to a granddad:

You are
an open flower
in the sunlight.
Without you
I would be
a dead rose . . .

I listen at night and I cannot hear him bark

Tymnes (2nd century BC), trans. ER and FS

'Thinking about death!' somebody said to me: 'They're only children. How morbid!' But 'in the midst of life we are in death', and sometimes it comes close to them, as it does to us. Asked to write about 'an impossible but beautiful thing' to put in her box (see Idea 19), Angela wrote 'My Uncle Terry, who died last Thursday', and burst into tears. The children hugged her, as did her teachers (this was allowed then, about 15 years ago). It is wicked if we do not allow children time to think about one experience that we all will have.

It is best to start with the deaths of animals. Here is a poem from the Ancient Greek of Tymnes (2nd century BC). The translators have brought it up to date and set it in England (Battersea Dogs' Home is a London institution where you can collect a stray dog).

A BATTERSEA DOG

We got him in Battersea twelve years since.
We loved his bark and the symmetrical prints
Of his paws
On shiny floors
But last week the dark chose him, or he chose the dark.
I listen at night and I cannot hear him bark.

(version by ER and FS)

Ask the children to think hard about a dog or cat they have lost through death: first, about the pet itself, its looks, its sounds, its behaviour, and ways in which, perhaps, it differed from other dogs and cats. Then ask them to think about their relationship with the pet: what games they played with it, and how they looked after it.

Finally, you might ask, what were your feelings about its death? Can you imagine its feelings, as it realized it was going to die? And the feelings of animals when their owners die? What happens to an animal when it dies? The thinking will lead to discussion.

THINKING ABOUT DEATH: ANIMALS

REMEMBERING

But of course, death affects us much more when human beings, and not just animals, die.

This lesson needs great sensitivity, and teachers shouldn't try it unless they know a class well. It is also best done in small groups, rather than in a class setting. If you are squeamish about this subject, remember that a curriculum that fails to help bereaved children is one that lets children down.

Ask children to collect memories of grandparents and grandparents who have died. Tragically, they will sometimes have memories of parents, and even siblings, who have died. Ask them to write about some of the memories.

Sometimes this isn't a lesson at all. A child who is distressed at school because of the death of someone close to him might well be comforted by the opportunity to write, working one-to-one perhaps with a learning support assistant.

This story has been adapted from *100 Ideas for Primary Assemblies* by Fred Sedgwick.

When Hannah was small, her grandfather had played football with her in the winter, and cricket in the summer. The lawn was worn bare in patches where Hannah had saved granddad's shots in the winter, and batted and bowled in the summer.

But now Grandfather was too old to play in the garden. He mostly sat in his armchair, reading. Sometimes he read to Hannah.

Hannah and her granddad loved cacti. Grandfather had been collecting them for many years, and when she was seven, Hannah had started to help with the collecting, and with the looking after.

She helped him to re-pot the ones that needed more soil and more space for their roots. When she took them out of the old pot, the roots were all tangled and squashed. She thought of them in their new bigger pots, and imagined them saying, 'Ah, that's better, I can stretch out now . . .'

The sunny room where they kept the cacti was full of them. There were tiny ones that grew a little bigger as each year went by. There were knobbly yellow ones. And there was one that flowered in great pinkish-red flames every winter.

Hannah often whispered the names to herself: 'Hedgehog cactus, silver torch cactus, sunset cactus, old man cactus . . .'

Hannah's parents used to watch Granddad and Hannah pottering in the sunny room, and smile bright smiles. Sometimes they took photographs, and pinned them on the wall of the sunny room.

But the old man was getting weaker. On some days, he only got out of bed for a few hours. Then, they would read to each other in the bedroom, the old man lying in the bed, the girl lying on it.

The doctor came sometimes to see the old man, and to talk to Hannah's parents.

One day the old man didn't get up at all. Hannah knew that he was going to die.

Then the house was quiet for a few days.

HANNAH AND GRANDDAD

After her Granddad had died, Hannah looked at the cacti. They were sad now. But she was glad of them. She learned how to re-pot them by herself. Her parents used to watch her in the sunny room, with smiles on their faces – not bright smiles, but sad ones.

'I will never forget Granddad,' Hannah thought. 'He lives on in the sunny room where the cacti go on growing, and where Mum and Dad have put the photographs, and he lives in my head.' She whispered the names to herself again: 'Hedgehog cactus, silver torch cactus, sunset cactus, old man cactus . . .'

And at Christmas that year one of the cacti shot out its flamey flowers, brighter and larger than ever.

(FS)

Recap the story. Then ask some questions:

○ Where is Grandfather now?
  - He is in the grave, or in the smoke that curls from the crematorium
  - He is in Heaven
  - He is in Hannah's thinking and feeling
    He has eternal life
○ What does 'eternal' mean?
○ What will Hannah have to remember her grandfather by?
○ Has anyone any happy memories of a grandfather/grandmother/great-grandfather/great-grandmother?

WHERE IS GRANDDAD NOW?

I'm farther off from Heaven
Than when I was a boy

Thomas Hood

Read 'I remember, I remember' by Thomas Hood to the
children. It's in many anthologies, including my own *Will
there really be a morning?* (David Fulton Publishers).
Here's the first stanza:

> *I remember, I remember,*
> *The house where I was born,*
> *The little windows where the sun*
> *Came peeping in at morn.*
> *He never came a wink too soon*
> *Nor brought too long a day*
> *But now I often wish the night*
> *Had borne my breath away . . .*

Ask the children to write about memories. Here is
Christopher's. I must tell you something about him. He
had been labelled as a child with learning difficulties. His
spelling reveals some of them – he spelt 'remember' right
only because I had made a thing about it. His lines also
reveal his local dialect ('da'). But what thinking, and
what feeling there is in these lines:

> *I remember*
> *when I was nearly eight yers old*
> *I found out that my da died*
> *in hospital me and my famly*
> *had to live without him*
> *I felt*
> *lost*
>
> *I remember*
> *when I was nealy eight yers old*
> *my dad was alive*
> *I youst to play with him*
> *I felt*
> *happy then*
>
> *I remember*
> *when I was eight yers old*
> *when my dad hifi came on*

when I never tuched it
it was
strange

The placing, intentional or not, of the words 'lost' and 'strange' is moving and articulate. So is the unexplained mystery in the last stanza. And there is no sentimentality (that is, emotion in excess of the facts) in the lines. And remember, Christopher had been labelled as a child with learning difficulties.

Ask the children to write a poem about someone they loved who has died, beginning 'I remember'.

BRAIN-SHOWERING

Tell the children: we have a problem. How are we going to solve it? This is best done in groups of between five and twelve. One person is put in the chair. Another is asked to act as secretary, and to write notes about the suggestions.

The rules are that nobody may criticize anyone else's suggestion until everybody's have been heard, and that everyone must be heard out.

Here are some suggested problems:

o There is not enough play space on the school grounds. How can we improve things?
o Most of the boys and a few girls dominate the playground with football. How can we make things fairer for everyone: the rest of the girls, smaller children, and boys who don't like football?
o Some children like quiet, both outside and inside. How can we provide it for them?
o How should we deal with bullying? How should we deal with insults, especially racist insults?
o At assembly, the first class has to wait ten minutes for the last to arrive. How can we stop this waste of time?

Each group should report back to the rest of the class and, later, if it is appropriate, to the whole school in assembly.

Ask the children to think about hypothetical situations. Here are some headlines.

PLASTIC BAGS ILLEGAL FROM NEXT WEEK
What would happen? For example, the amount of litter would decline. There would be no nasty plastic flags hanging from trees alongside big roads. There would be a positive effect on the earth's waste of fossil fuels (children should research this).

But how would we carry shopping home? And what about the jobs of the people who make them? What other skills might be invented or re-invented to make environment-friendly bags?

Children should ask grandparents: how did you carry your shopping home?

TELEVISION ADVERTISING: ALL CHILDREN'S TOYS, ESPECIALLY AT CHRISTMAS, BANNED
Good news: parents will spend less at Christmas, and be better off in the new year. Producers won't be able to exaggerate the quality of their products.

Bad news: Children won't get all the toys they want for Christmas. And there won't be enough information to help us compare different products.

ALL ADVERTISING BANNED
Dangerous products – junk food, alcohol, tobacco – couldn't be advertised. But would this make any difference to the consumption of junk food, alcohol and tobacco? And how would we find out about which new car goes fastest on less petrol, which new gel keeps our hair in place more effectively, and what toothpaste makes our teeth whiter?

And what about jobs in the advertising industry?

NEW TECHNIQUE: WE WILL BE ABLE TO SEE WHAT EVERYONE IS THINKING, SCIENTISTS SAY
What effects would this have on:

o Parties
o Life in classrooms
o In class
o Everywhere?

WE WILL BE ABLE TO SEE SMELLS AS COLOURS

This can either be a brain-showering exercise in a small group, or it can be done as a class activity. When ideas have been presented, and someone has recorded them, ask the children to arrange them into good results and bad results.

I am simply calling attention to the fact that fine art is the only teacher except torture

George Bernard Shaw

I quote Shaw's hyperbole because the National Curriculum barely acknowledges the teaching power of fine art at all.

There are several approaches to looking at pictures, all of them relevant to children and their thinking. Among them are:

○ Technical: how has the artist achieved this effect? Look at brushstrokes, for example.
○ Composition and colour: Why has the artist chosen these colours? What mood do they convey? Why has he or she placed that object where he or she has? What are our eyes drawn to when we first look at the picture? Look at the light and dark. Where does the light in the picture come from?
○ Historical and narrative: What do you think is going on in this picture? Can you place the period in history?
○ What do the clothes and furnishings tell you?

The following ideas are based on art postcards. I have been collecting these little rectangles, so useful and so cheap, both for my personal use, and for use in schools for many years, although it is important to say here that looking at any reproduction is no substitution for looking at the real thing.

(I concentrate below and in the next few ideas on pictures that were part of the Sainsbury's 'Art in Schools' scheme in 1995, because they exist in reproduction form in many schools. Decently framed reproductions of them were spread widely around the UK. I wonder sometimes how often children are allowed to look at, let alone study, these pictures. I see them still, after all these years, in school entrance halls and corridors, with children and teachers and parents passing them by. They are nothing but decoration. Sometimes they are stored away in the men's lavatories. They are worth more than that.)

'TWO BOYS AND A GIRL MAKING MUSIC' BY JAN MOLENAER

Ask the children to spend one minute looking at the Molenaer. Then ask them:

- ○ What are the main colours in this picture?
- ○ Which colour stands out as different?
- ○ What are the children using to make their music?
- ○ Are the children wealthy children? Give reasons for your view.
- ○ How would you describe the expressions on the children's faces?
- ○ What are they wearing?
- ○ What is the connection between what the girl is wearing around her neck, and what she is playing?
- ○ Where might she have found these things?
- ○ If this picture could make noises, what would you hear?
- ○ Write down some words that come to mind when you look at this picture. Begin with war, smiles, noise, and go on from there.

Ask the children to look again for two minutes, then put the questions to them again. They should have noticed new things.

I'm in the National Gallery now, making notes in front of this picture. They say: 'Nearly everything is beige and fawn except for the tunic (?) on the boy on the right. Scarlet for him. Are they celebrating something? The end of a war? That helmet. Why has the boy on the right taken his shoes off? He rests his feet on a box. One child has a real instrument, a fiddle, but the girl bangs on a helmet with cutlery, the boy scrapes his music – it's a rommel box! Why is there a cage far left? Why is there a golf club?'

Children could go to the National Gallery, and make their notes. Or sit in front of the reproduction in class, and make them there. They might look through a book of reproductions of pictures made after 1700, and count how many depict only children. There are very few. What does this tell us about the way society viewed children?

'ORTHODOX BOYS' BY BERNARD PERLIN

Again, the children should look at the picture for at least one silent minute. Then ask them:

○ Describe what the boys are wearing.
○ Describe the expressions on their faces.
○ What's behind them? What might the boys be thinking? Look at their faces, especially at the boy on the left.
○ What do you think the red book is about? What might be in the boy's hands?
○ What are the main colours in this picture? (The black of their caps and the darkness of their clothes both contrast with the green of the wall.)
○ Get some of the children to come out and examine closely the writing on the wall. What can they find?

This could well lead into a discussion about prejudice. The boys are Orthodox Jews, and easily recognizable as such. They are wearing yarmulkes, or skull caps. Some of the graffiti is anti-Semitic. Ask the children to find out more about anti-Semitism.

Ask the children to give the picture two more concentrated minutes.

A MODERN PICTURE

'THE WOODMAN'S DAUGHTER' BY JOHN EVERETT MILLAIS

Ask the children to compare the clothes of the two children: what is the boy doing? Why might he be doing that?

There are some strange things in this painting: ask them to look carefully at the boy's right arm, the girl's head, and how the artist has painted the ferns.

Sensitive questions here will give rise to questions about class. What is the job of the girl's father? What do the boy's clothes suggest about *his* father?

Culture is acquainting ourselves with the best that has been known and said in the world, and thus with the history of the human spirit.

Matthew Arnold

All the pictures I have referred to are in London, at the National Gallery in Trafalgar Square, except for 'Orthodox Boys', which is at the Tate Britain Gallery on Millbank. So they are accessible to thousands of children.

Every major city, and many a town, has a gallery where pictures are waiting to be viewed, and any teacher who has eyes ready to look can find things which will help, both with their own thinking, and with their children's. I have listed galleries that I have visited, and a few others:

- Belfast: Ormeau Baths Gallery
- Birmingham Museums and Art Gallery
- Brighton Museum and Art Gallery
- Bristol: Arnolfini
- Cambridge: Fitzwilliam Museum
- Cardiff: National Museum and Gallery
- Edinburgh: National Galleries of Scotland
- Gateshead: Baltic Centre for Contemporary Arts
- Glasgow: City Museums
- Huddersfield Art Gallery
- Leeds Metropolitan University Gallery
- Leicester: City Gallery
- Liverpool: Tate Gallery
- Manchester Art Gallery
- Newcastle: Laing Art Gallery
- Norwich: Sainsbury Centre for Visual Arts
- Nottingham: Yard Gallery
- Salford: The Lowry
- Salisbury Arts Centre
- Southampton: John Hansard Gallery
- Southampton: Millais Gallery
- St Ives: Tate Gallery
- Sunderland: Northern Gallery of Contemporary Art
- York Art Gallery

Looking closely at art feeds into all thinking. It can make children aware of history, family relationships, and symbolism. But it is also exhausting. Avoid a tiring trudge through hundreds of pictures. Before a visit to a gallery, ask the children to look out for one to five pictures that draw them in, and that interest them especially. Ask them to make notes about them, writing down:

○ The predominant colours
○ The expressions on faces
○ The background
○ The little objects around the edge of the picture
○ Random thoughts about those things.

Ask the children to look at books of reproductions in the same way, concentrating on a few pictures.

John Betjeman wrote that all towns are interesting: you only had to train yourself to look at the buildings carefully as you walked around, and you never would be bored. I have proved, to my own satisfaction at least, that this is true. There are many ways to help children to observe in towns.

Ask the children about the building in which they learn. This is the least interesting way, both because it is their school, and therefore familiar, and because it is likely to be a modern functional building.

Take them for a walk down a high street. Ask the children to 'look above the shops'. John Betjeman wrote (*First and Last Loves*) that the 'old High Street just peeps above the shop facades'. And he wrote that in 1952! It is even more true now.

Ask the children: Who lived or worked here before the shops were built? Ask them to record, on clipboards, in words and sketches, the shapes of windows, the materials (brick, stone, concrete).

Some of the children will be able to imagine what the parts of the buildings now hidden by shop facades may once have looked like. Some frontages have large rectangular windows on the first floor, and smaller windows on the upper floors. These are mostly Georgian. The smaller windows were needed upstairs because servants lived there, and they, it was thought, needed less light. Also, glass was expensive in Georgian times. What does that tell us about the relations between rich and poor at the time when these buildings were put up?

The shops weren't always shops. Find some old photographs of the town. What were these buildings put up for? Alternatively, you could find a building with a special purpose: a cinema, a place of worship, a bingo hall.

Whatever the building, here are some questions to ask:

o Why is that there?
o Why is it arranged like this?
o Where does the light come from?
o How are those walls held up?
o Can you count the shapes in the windows?

Find a building that is now redundant. I often work in Stratford in East London. Opposite one school is a derelict Victorian synagogue. Help the children to find other examples of decaying buildings, or buildings that have changed their purpose. Ask them to think: Why has this happened? What might this building be turned into? And why was there once a synagogue there? And why is it gone now?

Ask the children to think: How does the way a house is built tell us about how people live?

Why are bedrooms almost always upstairs? Is it because our ancestors slept in trees? How different would everyday life be if the kitchen, dining room and sitting room were upstairs, and the bedrooms and bathroom downstairs? Why not?

Find out which windows face east. Why do they face east? Is it to do with the sun? And why are certain colours likely to be chosen for, say, a living room or a dining room, and almost never for a bedroom or a bathroom?

How would the children decorate their bedroom if they had a free hand? Once they've gone through the inevitable images from popular culture, ask them to think about:

○ What colours are relaxing before you go to sleep?
○ Which ones might keep you awake?
○ What images do you want to have around to help you greet the morning cheerfully?

Ask the children to design the perfect house. They will have to make a frontal elevation drawing, and two plans, one for each floor.

The English may not like music – but they absolutely love the noise it makes.

Thomas Beecham, Conductor

I don't find listening to music helpful for thinking: I find it distracting. The rhythms get in the way and smudge my mind's work, and the emotions I hear in the music conflict with what I am thinking about.

But some people do find music helpful. They react in many different ways: In Howards End by E.M. Forster, the characters have different reactions to listening to Beethoven's Fifth Symphony. Not very musical Mrs Munt taps her foot when the tunes come. Passionate Helen sees heroes, shipwrecks, goblins and dancing elephants. Clever Tibby waits for the 'transitional drum passage'. Fraulein Mosebach 'remembers all the time that Beethoven is "echt Deutsch"'. Her young man can think of nothing but Fraulein Mosebach. When you listen to music, Forster comments, 'the passion of your life becomes more vivid'.

Play some non-vocal music, and ask the children: What does it make them think of? You can try:

o the slow movement of Schubert's String Quintet, or the Trout Quartet
o early jazz by Louis Armstrong
o a slow movement of a Mozart piano concerto
o the Fingal's Cave Overture by Mendelssohn
o any of the Planets movements by Holst
o The Ride of the Valkyries by Wagner.

Note that music that is familiar to the children will not work, because they already have their associations with it.

This activity is designed to help children to think divergently. Ask them to find a use for:

○ a brick
○ a deflated football
○ a coin (spending it is not allowed)
○ a disused ashtray
○ an empty film cartridge
○ an old dog leash
○ a CD that doesn't work anymore
○ last year's Christmas cards
○ an old paperback book that's coming to pieces
○ a broken umbrella
○ a nightmare
○ wooden garden furniture that has collapsed.

For example, bricks can be used for building book, CD, DVD, or video shelves. An ashtray can be a candle holder. CDs and DVDs make sparkling mobiles hanging from trees: they catch the light as they turn. A broken umbrella, if it is black, makes a wounded bat, and a nightmare might get made into a poem. Broken garden furniture can be made into abstract sculpture.

USES FOR . . .

During any historical topic, ask the children the 'What if . . . ?' question.

Some examples:

○ What if the Vikings had not needed land that they could farm, and had therefore stayed in Scandinavia?

○ What if Henry VIII had had a son by his first wife Catherine of Aragon, and that son had survived, and gradually become a power in the land?

○ What if Columbus had missed America?

○ What if Britain hadn't sent convicts to Australia?

○ What if the Gunpowder Plot had succeeded?

○ What if the slave trade had not started?

○ What if Florence Nightingale had not gone to the Crimea?

○ What if the Ancient Egyptians hadn't invented the process of mummification?

○ What if beer hadn't been invented?

○ What if Harold had won the Battle of Hastings?

○ What if the Romans had never come to Britain?

Geography is about maps,
But Biography is about chaps

E.C. Bentley

To think about geography, of course, is to think about rather more than maps. It is to think about, among other things, the world, and what its earth and seas give up when humankind works on them. Even more, it is to think about both the people who harvest and produce those resources, and the people who consume them.

Children can begin thinking about geography as they wander around the supermarket: where does their food come from? Ask them to look at the labels on fruit, meat and vegetables: where has this packet of blueberries come from? And this plastic-covered packet of apples? And this packet of tea and this packet of coffee? They will find the names of many countries, but they will have to look closely, because the information will almost certainly be given in small print. Ask the children to find out about Fairtrade products.

Ask them to find as many products as they can that have been grown in the United Kingdom. Sometimes, these foods have the union flag printed on them. They should then bring the results of their researches into the classroom, and talk about them.

Locate the countries for which these goods have been important in an atlas or on a globe. How many airmiles were covered to bring those blueberries, those apples, that New Zealand lamb to the UK . . . ?

THINKING ABOUT SCIENCE

Three definitions from the *Longmans Dictionary*:

Physics: *'a science that deals with . . . matter and energy in such fields as mechanics, heat, electricity, magnetism, atomic structure etc'*
Chemistry: *'a science that deals with the composition, structure and properties of substances and of the changes they undergo' (adapted)*
Biology: *'a science that deals with . . . the life processes of living organisms'.*

At the end of a school day, find out what the children know about biology, physics and chemistry. Ask them, during the evening, to check which of these sciences is providing them with the necessities of life. For example, which is it when they turn a light on or off, fetch something to eat from the fridge, watch television or a DVD, eat tea or breakfast, and drink milk or cocoa? What about their bodily functions? What about cooking, from making a cup of tea or coffee to frying, boiling, roasting and baking meat and vegetables?

What knowledge of botany have they used to identify plants in a garden, or trees on the way home from or back to school? What natural phenomena have they observed in the sky? And zoology? What animals have they seen or heard or smelt (or eaten!)?

Here are very young children learning some natural philosophy. The children had balloons that had been filled with water and left in a freezer overnight. The teacher put them in the sink, and the children played with them, feeling, looking, stroking, poking, watching, and talking. It would be impossible to be four years old and not think philosophically about that obsession of the Ancient Greeks – change.

I wrote down some of the things that they said:

'They're cold, rock-hard freezing things . . . melty on the outside . . . They're squeezy, slippery things, soggy and squidgy . . . the rubber split and peeled off and we felt them again . . . small windows on the ice . . . rainbow bubbles bubbling and popping and lines inside and lights . . . they looked like moons and they melted in our hands . . .'

A SCIENCE EXPERIMENT IN THE NURSERY

THINKING ABOUT PHYSICAL EDUCATION: BEFORE THE LESSON

Teachers think about why they are teaching children to do certain things in a PE lesson. But do the children ever have a chance to think about these things too? As a basic example, in the classroom, after a long assembly, we might ask the children to stretch before we ask them to listen to instructions. We do this (or I do) because they need oxygen, they need the blood to flow, and they need energy to move around their system, because they've had too much time being static already.

So before the PE session, tell the children what they will be doing in the lesson. In other words, will the lesson be about balance, speed, control, climbing (or whatever)? Ask them before going to the gym or the playground: why will we be doing this? For example: Why do we run in a lesson on the playground? Because it's fun. But also?

If they don't bring it up, talk about fitness; about the heart, and getting its beat up to 120 beats per minute a few times every day. Ask the children to do some research on the heart.

In the lesson, as they wait (briefly – there is too much sitting in many PE lessons) to start, ask the children about the previous conversation. Tell them that good gymnasts don't only use their bodies. They also use their brains. This is a surprise to some children, who, unconsciously or not, see PE merely as a time to relax mentally. They have to be taught that the brain never stops working. They need to be more aware of its working, and make that working more fluent and active.

Ask them to think when they run. They must be thinking of paths in the hall where they will not collide with each other. Ask them to think when they balance, or jump. Are the shapes they are making neat and good-looking, or untidy and ugly? Ask them to watch each other running, balancing and jumping. What can they learn from each other?

Halfway through the lesson, ask the children to think again: How different does the body feel now, after the exercise? How can I improve the movements I made?

Ask the children: What is the aim of games? Here are some possible answers:

o To produce winners for our country when we perform in the World Cup or in the Olympics.
o To get fit, and to stay fit.
o To beat the nearest school.

What others are there?
Ask them to imagine what goes through the mind of:

o a cricketer, as he or she faces a fast bowler
o a midfield footballer, as he or she receives the ball and looks up
o a tennis player, as he or she prepares to serve, or to receive a serve.

Cricketers, football players and tennis players have a particular kind of intelligence that they work at developing, involving speed of perception.

If a man will begin with certainties, he shall end in doubts; but if he be content to begin with doubts, he shall end in certainties

Francis Bacon, *Advancement of Learning*

'How did the space–time continuum begin?'

6-year-old

It is a truism that we shouldn't underestimate what children can achieve. I have developed one of my favourite lessons as an attempt to push them as far as possible in their thinking, and I've done it with the whole school range, from 5-year-olds to upper secondary age. I call this lesson 'philosophical questions'. Because it is the central part of this book, it uses up five ideas.

I write up on the board 'philo' and explain that it means 'friend' or 'lover' in Ancient Greek. Then I write 'sophy' up. This, I explain, means 'knowledge', or 'wisdom' in the same language. When we put the two together, we get 'philosophy', which means friendship with, or lover of, knowledge.

I then say: 'We are going to do philosophy now. We are going to be friends with knowledge: philosophers. We are interested in questions, not answers. Please close your eyes, and think of a question you'd love to know the answer to, but you know you never will. It mustn't be a question you could look up in a book, or on the internet. Even your teacher doesn't know the answer! . . .When you've thought of one, put your hand up.'

As their hands begin to go up – that is, as they stop thinking, and start competing – I say: 'When you've got one question, keep your eyes closed and your hands down, and think of another . . . and another . . . and another.'

This thinking time . . . how important it is. And how rare it is . . .

After about two minutes, many of them will be dying to share questions. I did this the other week, and the first question came from a 6-year-old boy: 'How did the space–time continuum begin?'

Spend some time listening to what the children have thought up.

In the next lesson, I ask the children to close their eyes again, and think of more questions, containing words like 'peace', 'love', 'hate', 'war', 'good' and 'evil'.

Among the most striking questions children have asked have been (all from 6-year-olds) 'How can I tell if a man is evil or not?' and (variations of this almost always come up) 'Why do we die?' And this came from a 9-year-old girl of Singaporean extraction in a Catholic school: 'My granddad didn't believe in Jesus. Will I meet him in Heaven?'

Reflect for a moment. She said that, now, in her classroom. How many hours had she spent in bed worrying about it, without any chance to express her worries?

Again, share these questions.

6-year-old

In another lesson, I read the children the questions that they have written down. I ask the children to think of further questions with words like 'God' in them: 'dos god bleeve in me' (no, I didn't correct spelling and grammar) is my personal favourite.

In the next lesson, point out to the children that their thinking has provoked important questions about big things. Produce large printouts of the questions, and, with the help of the children and the learning support assistant, discussing as you do so the best ways to make the display look eye-catching and attractive, stick them up on the wall. Put up a label saying 'WE HAVE BEEN ASKING PHILOSOPHICAL QUESTIONS': first, to remind the children what they have been doing, and how hard they have thought; second, to celebrate philosophy; and third, to baffle any passing inspector.

MORE PHILOSOPHICAL QUESTIONS

PHILOSOPHICAL QUESTIONS:
WRITE THEM DOWN

Ask the children to write down their most interesting
questions in any way they like:

o In a prose sequence older children could be asked to
   group their questions in paragraphs:
   o questions about the universe
   o questions about love
   o questions about religion
   o questions about death
   and so on . . .
o As a poem, repeating their most interesting question
   every four lines.
o As a letter to someone: a grandparent, or God, or the
   headteacher. For example, 'Dear God, I was
   wondering about these things . . . '.

This idea makes a brilliant assembly. Each child in your class reads his or her most interesting question. The school is then asked to go through the same process, but on a shorter timescale: 'Please close your eyes, and think of a question you'd love to know the answer to, but you know you never will . . .', and so on . . . The adults should be involved in this process. The children won't do what teachers all too often do: engage in mild sexist banter on the lines of 'Why can't women read maps?' and 'Why can't men wash saucepans up?' Discourage this.

A PHILOSOPHICAL ASSEMBLY

IDEA
74

This session goes back to the bedrock of western philosophy. The Ancient Greek Empedocles, who lived from about 490 to about 430 BC, believed that everything was made up of four elements: earth, air, fire and water. Whatever developments have taken place in our thinking about matter, this idea still has a strong grip on our minds.

Ask the children to imagine a famous person, either from history or the present day, of whom everyone in the class is likely to have heard: a king, queen, soldier, sailor, writer, artist, singer, sports person, politician . . . anyone. But they must be famous. Ask the children: If your person was weather, what weather would he or she be? Discourage one-word answers: not just sun, but 'a bright sun with fluffy clouds'; not just thunder, but 'a thunderstorm on a winter night' and so on.

Then ask them what animal their person would be. Again, ban one-word answers: the children could say what the animal's behaviour is like, or something about its habitat. 'He is a mole, secret and nervous', for example. Or, 'She is a raging lion, looking for antelopes.' Get them to write their answers down. Then ask the following questions:

○ What growing thing would your person be?
○ What item of furniture?
○ What music?

Think of other questions too: but all these are dry runs for the big question. Say: Your person is mostly made up of two or three of the elements, earth, air, fire or water. Which two? Ask them to give reasons for their answers. 'My person is air and water because . . .' (The word 'because' nearly always widens the path for more thinking, because it is essentially asking for evidence.)

Children read their sentences out, and the other children, and you, have to try to work out who they were thinking of and writing about. Insist that the children hear each other out to the last word before putting their hands up: they must, in other words, collect all the evidence.

Here is one child writing, it turned out, about Nelson Mandela:

> *He is a bright sunshine, and the terrible clouds have drifted away. He is a lion, but a kind and just one. He is a scarlet rose in a handsome garden. He is a throne that he shares with his people. He is fire and water because he fights for justice. His fire is hot when he is angry, light when he is free . . .*

Children reading aloud! This presents a problem in some schools, because nobody has coached children in a few simple techniques.

First, explain that their task, when they read out, is to communicate. If they think, or even philosophize, they will usually want to convey their thoughts, or their philosophizing, to other people. How will they communicate best while reading aloud? Here are some rules. They:

- Will read their writing through two or three times first, to iron out any problems in spelling or handwriting. And then they will read it again, but aloud, to themselves, and then to a friend. All this means that they will be familiar with their writing when they read it to the class. Not to be familiar with it, and therefore to stumble over words, is to show bad manners.
- Will take a deep breath before they start, and again whenever they reach a full stop, and sometimes when they reach a comma (or where a full stop, or a comma, should be).
- Will read slowly. Children do not understand, and neither do many adults, that the speed at which they read to themselves is not the same speed that they should use when reading aloud.

o Will look up at the audience whenever they have a chance.
o Will direct their voices at someone at the back of the room, probably an encouraging adult who is giving them full attention.
o Will hold the notebook or paper where they can see it properly, but not in front of their faces. They will not read with their paper on the desk, thereby aiming their voices downwards.

Now, ask the children to do this again with someone they like: mother, father or other carer; sister or brother; grandparents; teacher; best friend.

Again, practise communicating verbally by reading out the descriptions: first in pairs, then in groups, then to the whole class.

THE ELEMENTS: SOMEONE NOT FAMOUS

THE ELEMENTS: AN ANIMAL

Ask them to do this again with a pet (although leave out the animal question, obviously). For example:

> *My cat is earth because he loves the garden and what he might find.*
>
> *He was air once, when he leapt to catch birds, but now he is old. He is even more the earth now. He is an almost-still breeze because he is slow. He is fire when he bites me if I stroke him where he is tickled.*
>
> *He is never water! . . .*

Ask the children to read out their writing, using the rules already given. They will communicate better after 30 minutes' training in reading skills, given in three ten-minute bursts at the end of thinking sessions. This will improve the children's reading out loud within a week. If you continue to reinforce these skills for a term, this reinforcement will improve their vocal communication for ever, and hence their social skills. Please note that here, 'skills' is, for once, something like the right word.

Now do the exercise about yourself. One headteacher bravely wrote the following with a class:

I was once a spring morning, but am now an autumn afternoon.

I am still a hummingbird in the mornings, but a tortoise in the afternoon.

There is still fire in my heart, but it burns low. I can see the earth close from where I stand . . .

'WHAT IS TRUTH?'

The truth is rarely pure and never simple

Oscar Wilde

A truth that's told with bad intent
Beats all the lies you can invent

William Blake

Ask the children: Is it ever right to lie?

Name some times when it is clearly wrong (there should be a long list here). Then name some times when it is right to lie, using the examples from Idea 12:

o A family harbouring a Jewish family in Nazi Germany approached at night by the Gestapo.
o The woman who lied about her premature child's birthdate to get the necessary health care.

Ask the children to write down two lists of lies that they have told: one of lies that they don't regret telling, the other of lies that they do regret. Tell them that they can keep these lists secret.

Name some lies that are in the middle.

Are all truths told for good reasons? Can you imagine what the poet William Blake means when he writes: 'A truth that's told with bad intent'?

Here is a story, ancient as Richard Lionheart. It's about Robin Hood and Little John.

> *Robin was alone in the forest. He would only blow his horn to call his men if he met trouble.*
>
> *He came to a fallen tree trunk that lay across a river. He stepped on to one end of the trunk to cross, but a shout from the other side of the river jolted him. He looked up. A giant of a man, holding a huge staff, stood on the other side. The man shouted again.*
>
> *'Out of my way,' the man bellowed in a voice that was as large as himself, a voice like thunder. 'I am crossing this bridge.' Robin looked at the man, thought for an instant – and laughed.*
>
> *'No, you get out of my way,' he shouted back. The man laughed too. 'You seem to be sure you can make me move. Would you like to try?'*
>
> *Robin took from the quiver on his back a single arrow, and flexed his bow. He aimed it at the giant's heart.*
>
> *'Hey!' roared the big man. 'I have a staff here, and you would come at me like a coward with a bow and arrow?'*
>
> *Robin thought for a moment, and then laid his bow and arrow aside, and picked up a branch from the stream's edge. Quickly, he cut at it until it was a reasonable weapon, a stick. 'All right,' he shouted. 'I'll fight you with this, and whoever thumps the other into the stream is the winner.'*
>
> *They started smashing at each other. The sounds of wood on bone and flesh resounded through the glade. Then the giant's staff landed on Robin's head.*
>
> *And Robin fell into the river, and a trickle of scarlet from his head flowed away, quickly changing into a stream like a tattered ribbon . . .*
>
> *The big man laughed. 'Where are you now, you brave fellow?'*
>
> *'You are stronger,' said Robin, pulling himself out of the stream. 'You are a better battler. I'll fight no more. The fight is over.' Then, when he had his breath back, he took his horn, and blew a piercing blast on it.*
>
> *His bowmen, all dressed in green, were at his side at*

WOOD AND BONE ON FLESH: VIOLENCE

once. 'What's the matter Robin? Why all this blood?
Why are you soaking wet?' Their eyes turned to the big
man, and they made a circle around him. 'Shall we
throw him in the stream?', they asked. 'No,' said
Robin. 'He is a brave true man, and he shall join us.'
And the big man said Robin was brave, too, and joined
his Merry Men in the forest. And because his name
was John Little, they called him Little John.

(Version FS)

Ask the children these questions:

o Was this violence justified?
o How could it have been avoided?
o How did the two men resolve their difference?
o What was their attitude to each other after the fight?

Many believers in eastern religions are taught that all violence is wrong. Ask the children to research Jainist and Hindu pacifism.

Jesus sometimes appears to be pacifist. He says at one point that when someone hits us we should 'turn the other cheek', and, just before his death, he heals a man whom Peter, his disciple, has wounded. But somewhere else he says that he came 'not to bring peace but a sword'.

Headteachers tell us that violence is always wrong, and they have the best reasons for saying this. What do you think are those reasons? But when might violence be right? How about:

○ Defending a defenceless person being attacked on the pavement?
○ When a tyrant kills his people and threatens the safety of the world? Should we take arms against him?

VIOLENCE: IS IT EVER RIGHT?

Are children ever asked to think about their own
playground violence? This poem is about that:

THE FIGHT

> There's a fight on the playground today.
>   Two big boys from Mr Magee's
> Are knocking the daylights out of each other
>   Under the trees.
>
> The girls are silent and staring
>   And Clare whispers 'Stop it Paul'
> As the fighting gets wilder, and feet jab out
>   And fingers maul.
>
> I watch, and I'm glad it's Joe
>   And not me in that horrible space,
> Not my nose bleeding, not my stomach winded
>   Not my burning face.
>
> The sky is bright. Two planes fly
>   Out from the base, while one
> Boy holds the other down with his knee
>   And breathes, 'You done?'
>
> There's a fight on the playground today.
>   Paul Topple from Mr Magee's
> Is crushing the daylights out of Joe Randall
>   Under the trees.

(FS)

I asked a group of 9-year-olds what they could say when
they had the problem that a fight was coming. They
didn't know the word 'problem', and I explained it to
them. This suggested to them that if there was a
problem, there is, very likely, a solution; probably more
than one. They talked about different times when they
wanted to fight, and what the problem was, and how
they might find the solution and prevent a fight.

For some teachers, work on the negative emotions, like work on death, raises questions. Will a lesson about violence that is true to its subject make some children violent? Or will a lesson about anger bring out a potentially angry child's fury? On the contrary, this is a subject better talked about, written about, than bottled up.

This is my poem about a very young child's tantrum, seen from her point of view.

I SCREAMED AT MY MUMMY

When I was angry
I screamed at my mummy.

I was quiet
for a long long time.

I curled up
in her arms

and said 'Sorry'
and she said

'That's all right
My little Chickadee'

and then she tickled me.

(FS)

I ask young children, from nursery up to 8 years old: What makes you angry? What do you feel like inside when you are angry?

Ask the children to explore their heads when they were angry – in other words, to reflect in tranquillity what the turmoil was like. Ask them to draw the inside of their heads when they are angry.

ANGER: TELLING IT

I told it not, my wrath did grow

William Blake

For older children, here is a famous, disturbing poem by William Blake:

I was angry with my friend:
I told my wrath, my wrath did end.
I was angry with my foe:
I told it not, my wrath did grow.

And I water'd it with fears,
Night and morning with my tears;
And I sunned it with smiles,
And with soft deceitful wiles.

And it grew both day and night,
Till it bore an apple bright,
And my foe beheld it shine,
And he knew that it was mine,

And into my garden stole
When the night had veil'd the pole:
In the morning glad I see
My foe outstretched beneath the tree.

Ask the children: how many times does the word 'and' appear? If you read the poem emphasizing this little word, some of the children will appreciate how it makes the poem gather pace, and how it makes the poem ominous and urgent.

Look how many times the words 'angry' and 'wrath' appear in the first stanza. This is a very angry man, and he gets angrier as the poem proceeds . . .

Look at the adjective 'glad' in the last stanza: 'In the *morning* glad *I* see'. There are two possible nouns for this adjective to qualify, or more accurately, one noun and one pronoun. Can the children identify them? It's both the morning, and the speaker ('I'). Explain that, in Blake's time, it was conventional sometimes to put the adjective after a noun instead of before it.

Can the children find a story about an apple that was dangerous? There's one involving a mirror and a stepmother.

Tell the children about a time when you were frightened.
Here's a story where fear is the main character.

Grandfather and Hannah had both grown up in towns. They loved the noise of traffic. It was part of their lives.

But now they were staying in the countryside. Hannah's parents had booked a two-week holiday in a little cottage. They were 'miles', as they kept saying, 'from anywhere'. The cottage had no phone.

And Grandfather and Hannah were loving that, too. It was quiet: from her bedroom in the morning, all Hannah could hear was birdsong. She ate her breakfast, and listened to the quiet.

And, at night, she could see the stars.

One afternoon, Grandfather said, 'I'll take you out to a dance tonight. We'll go to a barn dance at the church hall in the village, and Mum and Dad can have an evening doing what they want.'

All evening, Grandfather and Hannah danced. Hannah danced with the children from the local school, and made friends with some of them. Grandfather danced with the vicar's wife.

It was dark when they began their walk home. Both of them were startled by how navy blue everything was. It was clear, and they could see the stars. She felt she could learn to know them, so clear they were. Grandfather pointed out the hunter and the plough.

(You could show the children diagrams of these constellations, and ask them to look for them on a clear night before bedtime. They figure later in this book.)

The moon was full, and it cast a ghostly light on everything.

As they walked away from the church hall, a cloud drifted over the moon, and the night became darker. But Hannah didn't mind, as she marched along the road holding her grandfather's hand.

They turned off the road, and onto the path to the cottage. The moon disappeared. Now it was very dark indeed, and Hannah felt nervous. They continued

A GHOSTLY LIGHT

walking. They climbed a stile. They crossed a cattle grid. The path on the other side went across a field.

Then Hannah stopped. Ahead of them was a black, smooth shape. It seemed to make a sound like a ghost escaping, a great sigh, deep and terrible. Grandfather stopped too.

'What is it?' whispered Hannah.

'I don't know,' said her grandfather.

Hand in hand, they crept closer to the shape, which seemed to be in their way.

It made its great sigh again. They found they could walk past it, but they would be very close to it.

Grandfather laughed, suddenly. Very quietly.

'What is it?' Hannah asked, still scared.

'It is, my little treasure' said Granddad, 'it is – a cow.'

In the morning, Grandfather said to Mum and Dad, 'Last night we were frightened of a cow!'

'But', said Hannah, 'we'll never be frightened of one again, will we, Granddad?'

'No' said her grandfather.

There is, as we have seen, a problem with the word 'love' and a problem with the word 'think'. There are many words that present problems. Here are two more. Because they are problems, there may well be solutions.

Ask the children: What can we *know* and what can we *believe*?

Begin with certainties, such as the position of certain football teams in the league on a Sunday morning ('My team is fifth in the table') on the one hand, and the quality of those teams on the other ('City weren't any good'). Or, 'The sun rises in the east', contrasted with 'It will be a fine day'.

Ask them to divide a blank sheet into two columns. The left-hand column is for things we can know. Some of these things are useful, and some aren't. The right-hand column is for those that we cannot know but only believe. Some things might be written half-and-half in each column.

For examples, we *know*:

○ That everybody grows older at exactly the same rate
○ That the world is not made of butter
○ That if we have no oxygen, we die
○ That Nelson died during the battle of Trafalgar
○ That the field today is covered in sunlight (or rain, or mist, or snow, or whatever)
○ That violence hurts someone
○ That lies deceive someone.

On the other hand, we *believe*, or some of us do:

○ That Nelson was a great admiral (did all his officers believe that? And what about the enemy admirals?)
○ That all people are equal in the sight of God
○ That there is one God, and Allah is his name
○ That God was in Jesus (some people, of course, don't believe in God)
○ That the field in summer is a pleasant place (it isn't if you're in the middle of it, and lonely)
○ That violence and lying are wrong (are they? *Always?*).

IDEA

86

KNOWING AND BELIEVING

WORD TENNIS

This is a simple word game, to be played in any age group. It encourages quick thinking about the meanings of words. In a circle of five, the children appoint one child to the role of umpire. Subsequently, each child should take his or her turn in this part. Ask the first child to say a word. The second must say one that has a connection with the first. For example, with young children, the first word might be 'cat', the second 'fur', the third 'smooth'. Note, 'claws' would be wrong: although connected to 'cat', it is not necessarily connected to 'fur'. Or is it? The umpire decides, and his or her decision is, of course, final.

Older children might start with 'war', leading to 'battle', then to 'guns' and so on.

As the children grow in their understanding of words, they should play the game with abstract nouns. After a few goes with easy words, start one yourself with, say, 'love', 'peace', 'imagination' or 'hope'.

This is the same as above, but this time the word must NOT be connected to the previous one. For example: 'hat', 'begonia', 'pomegranate' and so on. This will become rowdy, and it must be made clear, again, that the umpire's decision is final.

If someone responded to 'head' with 'hat' or 'brain' or 'skull' it would obviously be wrong. But if someone responded to 'roof' with 'sky', it would be a matter for debate. You can see the sky against the roofs of the houses opposite.

ANTI-WORD TENNIS

THINKING ABOUT PREJUDICE

Ask the children to look this word up in different dictionaries, and to make notes of the definitions that they find.

The simple form of the etymology is easy: 'pre-' = before, 'judice' = judgement. To be prejudiced is to make a judgement about something – or, worse, someone – before we really know anything about that thing, or that person.

Then the children should look the word up in a thesaurus, and collect related words. 'Bias', 'bigotry', 'unfair' and 'one-sided' will all appear.

Talk about the words. Then, offer them some prejudiced remarks, for example:

o Children cannot understand difficult ideas.
o All old people are slow-witted and dull.
o Footballers are all yobs.
o British summers are awful.

Ask the children to discuss whether there is truth in them.

Next, ask the children what we mean by 'racist' and 'sexist' thinking and behaviour. With a class you know well, and where everyone is open about what I call 'hot' issues, children might be invited to offer examples of prejudice that they have encountered.

All we need to be philosophers is the faculty of wonder

'Wonder', says John Ayto in his *Dictionary of Word Origins*, 'is something of a mystery word.' All the Germanic languages have it: it's *wunder* in German, it's *undran* in Swedish and it's *undren* in Danish. But no one knows where it came from.

Tell the children this, and ask them: What does 'wonder' mean? Ask them to make some sentences up in which it is a verb, for example:

○ I wonder why the clouds on this summer night are wispy.
○ I wonder why the stars are there.
○ I wonder if there is a God.
○ I wonder how the universe began.

Now think of sentences where 'wonder' is part of an adjective. They will probably begin with 'I think it is wonderful when . . .', or 'It is a wonder that . . .'.

Ask them to think of something that is, right now, wonderful. For example:

○ A birth
○ A recovery from an illness
○ Some good news on the television, like peace where there was war, or a woman forgiving the person who killed her son.

Ask the children to write all their 'wonder' sentences, beginning a new line with each one, to make a 'wonder' poem.

IDEA 91

SALTY WORDS

Choose me,
You English words . . .

Edward Thomas

Looking hard at the origins of words can be useful for four reasons:

○ It gives pleasure to children who enjoy words.
○ It helps with spelling.
○ It can help us to understand a word better.
○ Most importantly, it helps us to realize the hugeness of the family of which we are a part.

Ask the children: What have salt, salad, sausages and salary in common? Well, we often put a little salt on sausages, and we may eat salad with them. Forget the salary for a moment.

Ask them to look at the words 'salt', 'salad' and 'sausages' closely. They all begin with the same two letters. So does salary, of course, but hold on . . .

All the words come from Latin. Salt (*sal*) was very important to the Romans. They didn't have fridges, and *sal* preserved their food. They made sausages with *sal*, and called them *salcicia*.★

The Romans kept their raw vegetables in *sal*, and called the dish *herba salita*, salted vegetables.

And salary? A Roman soldier was paid in salt, which was precious. It became his salary.

Somebody in your house probably earns a salary so you can eat sausages and salad with a little (not too much, now!) salt on them.

So 'salt', 'salad', 'sausages' and 'salary' are words that are related to each other. And we did not invent them. They came from Latin.

★Italians still have their *saliccia*.

For this the children need a decent etymological dictionary. It's almost certain to be an adult dictionary, because school dictionaries have nothing about word origins. Also useful is John Butterworth's *Word Origins* (which contains more in 32 pages than I would have believed possible), and the *Bloomsbury Dictionary of Word Origins* by John Ayto.

Languages form a family:

○ Indo-European is a great-granddad or a great-grandma
○ Celtic, Germanic, Latin, and Sanskrit are granddads or grandmas
○ West Germanic and North Germanic are mums or dads
○ Welsh, Irish and Gaelic are children of Celtic
○ English,* German and Dutch are children of West Germanic
○ Danish and Swedish are children of North Germanic
○ Italian, French, Spanish and Portuguese are children of Latin
○ Hindi, Urdu, Punjabi, Gujarati and Bengali are children of Sanskrit.

Ask the children to look up the words 'mother', 'father', 'sister' and 'brother' in a good dictionary, and find out where they came from. Then ask them to look at the following words, and (this is important) say them as well as they can: 'bhrater', 'frater', 'phrater', 'bhratr', 'brothar', 'bruder', 'broeder', 'broder'. Can they guess what the English equivalent is?

The words come from, in order: Northern India, Italy (Latin), Greece, India (Sanskrit), Germany (brothar and bruder), The Netherlands and Sweden. Find, in an atlas, all those countries.

The peoples in all these countries all have the same word (or very nearly) for 'brother'.

*Although, because of our history, we have many Latin words, too: remember that the Normans brought words to us, and also that the Romans had got many of their words from the Greek.

Indo-European

Celtic	**Germanic**		**Latin**	**Sanskrit**
	West	*North*		
Welsh	English	Dutch	Italian	Hindi
Irish	German	Swedish	French	Urdu
Gaelic	Dutch		Spanish	Punjabi
			Portuguese	Gujarati
				Bengali

Look up at the stars!

Gerard Manley Hopkins

Can the children find out what the letters 'astr' signify (think *astr*ology, and *astr*onomy)? '*Atar*' is Sanskrit, and '*astr*' is the Greek way of writing it. '*Stella*' is related (Latin) . . .

. . . and we have 'star'! A very old word. The French '*étoile*' may not sound like the other words, but it is related. So are the German '*Stern*', the Italian '*stella*', the Spanish '*estrella*' and even the Swedish '*stjarna*'.

Every man and woman, every boy and girl, has looked up at them as we do. Sanskrit speakers in India thousands of years ago, Greeks, Romans, and French, Germans and Swedes look up, and all use, essentially, the same word: variations of '*atar*'.

On a clear winter night, just before bedtime, spend some time looking at the sky. Find out the names of the con*stella*tions, or groups of stars. Note that *stella*, the Latin for star, is in that word.

Why is a great singer or actor or sportsperson called a 'star'?

IN MY BUNGALOW SHAMPOOING MY HAIR
WHILE WEARING MY PYJAMAS

Some words come from far away. Look up 'bungalow', and find the country where it comes from on the globe. It sounds rather like that country: say it to yourself.

And what about 'shampoo' and 'pyjamas'? They come from Hindi. 'Bungalow' comes from the word for Bengal. The British found single-storey houses there. What modern country does it sound like? Can the children find out why words from India came into our language in the eighteenth and nineteenth centuries?

There are words whose derivations we know nothing about. So invent derivations for these:

o Kick
o Dog
o Wonder
o Even
o Donkey
o Blizzard
o Badge

Here are two examples. My son suggests that 'kick' is onomatopoeic: it *sounds* like a kick. And is donkey derived from 'dun', a colour, and 'key', from a donkey's irritating noise? I think the 'zz' in blizzard sounds like the thing. Brrrrr! Your guesses are as good as ours.

Can the children think of words that are changing their meanings as they live? For example, what do they mean by 'wicked' and 'sick'? Even the latter, in some parts of the country, means 'excellent' to children.

To every thing there is a season
and a time to every purpose under the heaven:

A time to be born, and a time to die;
a time to plant, and a time to pluck up that which is
planted;

A time to kill, and a time to heal;
a time to break down, and a time to build up;

A time to weep, and a time to laugh;
a time to mourn, and a time to dance;

A time to cast away stones, and a time to gather stones
together;
a time to embrace, and a time to refrain from
embracing;

A time to get, and a time to lose;
a time to keep, and a time to cast away;

A time to rend, and a time to sew;
a time to keep silence, and a time to speak;

A time to love, and a time to hate;
a time of war and a time of peace.

These words offer so much to think about. We have no
choice about our time to be born, and our time to die;
but when is it a good time to kill? This includes killing
animals, and brings in issues about animal ethics,
including vegetarianism. When do we weep, and when do
we laugh? What helps us to stop weeping? Think about
laughter: what do we laugh at? Is some laughter unkind?
When do we mourn, and when do we dance? When
should we keep silence, and when should we speak? Is
there ever a right time for war?

Split the children into groups, and ask them to debate
these questions.

MY HEAD

God be in my head,
And in my understanding;

God be in my eyes,
And in my looking;

God be in my mouth,
And in my speaking;

God be in my head,
And in my thinking;

God be at my end,
And at my departing.

What word could be put in place of 'God' if we didn't believe in him? This could lead into a discussion about conscience, which comes from the Latin 'con', together, and 'science', knowledge.

I thank you, Lord, for knowing me
Better than I know myself,
And for letting me know myself
Better than others know me.

Make me, I ask you then,
Better than others know me.
Make me, I ask you then,
Better than they suppose,
And forgive me for what they do not know.

(Muslim prayer)

Ask the children about conscience.

Shalom, Sholem, Pace, Paz, Frieden, Fred, paix, pax, scholem

That's 'peace' in the following languages, in order: Hebrew, Arabic, Italian, Spanish, German, Danish (and Swedish), French, Latin, Yiddish.

Notice that the words from the Near East all begin with a 'sh' sound, the words from South Europe with a 'p' sound, and the words from the Germanic languages with an 'fr' sound. For once English has taken its word from the southern, from the Latin.

A child wrote of peace in her box writing (Idea 19). The children's grandparents will remember worrying about world peace at different times in their lives: when the Soviet leader Khrushchev and the USA president Kennedy stood nose to nose over the Bay of Pigs in 1961, and as the arms race accelerated in the 1960s and 1970s. Their parents will remember when the World Trade Centre was attacked in 2001, and many of the children will remember the attacks on the London transport system. The Iraq war will be in their minds now.

Children sleep uneasily sometimes, wondering whether the world they wake up to in the morning will be the world they saw when they went to bed, or whether it will be so different it is impossible to imagine: a world of war. Because they think in their random, fearful way about these things, it is our duty to address them in the classroom.

This lesson should begin with today's newspaper, where the opposite of peace is on prominent display. Leave newspapers around the classroom. Ask the children: Why do you think nations and peoples take to war? Is it:

○ Because they both want the same piece of land?
○ To protect resources?
○ Out of a sense of 'honour'?
○ Because their leaders believe that they should not let these people in another land, however distant, suffer?

PAX VOBISCUM – PEACE BE WITH YOU

111

Ask the children to talk about the victims in the papers. Then discuss the statement: 'Peace is more than the opposite of war.'

Here are two meditations on peace from the Hindu tradition:

O Lord lead me
From darkness to light, and
From death to immortality.
Let there be peace, peace and real peace.

(Diwali prayer)

May there be peace in the higher regions;
May there be peace in the firmament;
May there be peace on earth.
May the waters flow peacefully;
May all the divine powers bring us peace.
The supreme Lord is peace.
May we all be in peace, peace,
And only peace;

And may that peace
Come unto each of us.

Shanti – Shanti – Shanti

(From the Vedas)

Some of the children will enjoy *Sophie's World* by Jostein Gaarder. Ask them to find out:

o What philosophy is (pp 11–13, 14–17)
o What the Cynics believed (pp 109–10).

Ask the children who read the second passage to tell the other children the story of Diogenes' meeting with Alexander the Great. What are the main differences between Indo-European culture and Semitic culture (pp 125–39)?

What a lot of things I don't need

Socrates

Many thinkers have emphasized that wanting things is a cause of pain. Jesus pointed out that 'foxes have holes, and the birds of the air their nests, but the Son of Man has nowhere to lay his head'. Jesus, it seems, never lived in his own house. Socrates walked through the market and looked at the teeming stalls loaded with things that people were buying, and was heard to say, 'What a lot of things I don't need.'

Most Buddhists teach that suffering is caused by selfish craving. A baby is innocent of this need: at Christmas time parents, aunties, uncles, cousins, friends, godparents will bring her dozens of presents, but she will prefer to play with the wrapping paper.

Ask the children to make lists of things they don't have. Ask them to divide the list into two parts: things they need, and things that they want.

Have they ever yearned for things (toys at Christmas time, for example) and found them boring in a short while?

What is the good life? This has always been a central concern of philosophy. Ask the children to say what they would have and what they would do in their version of the good life.

This question itself should be enough to trigger a discussion about values. They may well begin with material benefits.

If the discussion doesn't go beyond this, the story of Midas will provoke seriously non-materialist thinking . . . (see my book *100 Ideas for Primary Assemblies*). King Midas prayed that everything he touched could be changed into gold, but soon found that he could no longer eat or drink or, worst of all, cuddle his beloved little girl . . .

See the good life in a negative way: In my good life, there will be no more . . .

See the good life in a positive way: In my good life I will . . .

THE GOOD LIFE

BIBLIOGRAPHY AND ACKNOWLEDGEMENT

Thanks to Peggy Cotton, for permission to quote two poems by her late husband and my late friend, John Cotton.

John Ayto (1990), *Bloomsbury Dictionary of Word Origins*. London: Bloomsbury.

John Butterworth (2001), *Word Origins*. Oxford: Oxford University Press.

David Crystal (2007), 'What's so special about Bricklehampton?' *Guardian*, 19 May.

Jostein Gaarder (1996), *Sophie's World: a novel about the History of Philosophy*. Trans. Paulette Moller. London: Phoenix.

Fred Sedgwick (2006a), *101 Essential Lists for Primary School Teachers*. London: Continuum Books.

Fred Sedgwick (2006b), *100 Ideas for Primary Assemblies*. London: Continuum Books.